28

Mock Tests

for

Olympiad

CLASS 2

Science | Mathematics | English
Logical Reasoning | GK | Cyber

DISHA™

Publication Inc

DISHA Publications Inc.

45, 2nd Floor, Maharishi Dayanand Marg,
Corner Market, Malviya Nagar, new Delhi –110017
Tel: 49842349/ 49842350

Typeset By

DISHA DTP Team

Buying books from DISHA

Just Got A Lot More Rewarding!!!

We at DISHA Publication, value your feedback immensely and to show our apperciation of our reviewers, we have launched a review contest.

To participate in this reward scheme, just follow these quick and simple steps:
- Write a review of the product you purchase on Amazon/Flipkart.
- Take a screenshot/photo of your review.
- Mail it to *disha-rewards@aiets.co.in*, along with all your details.

Each month, selected reviewers will win exciting gifts from DISHA Publication. Note that the rewards for each month will be declared in the first week of next month on our website.

https://bit.ly/review-reward-disha.

Write To Us At

feedback_disha@aiets.co.in

CONTENTS

English

Mathematics

Science

General Knowledge

Logical Reasoning

Cyber

Scan code to gain **FREE access** to **"Olympiad Champs"**, a unique page dedicated to prepare students of class 1-8 to ace all National Level Olympiad Exams.

Current Affairs Updates, Mock Tests, Past Papers, Quizzes, Interesting, Fun Facts, Parenting Articles & Free Courses

DISHA™ Publication Inc

ENGLISH MOCK TEST 1-5

OLYMPIAD Mock Test 1

Name : ___________

Max. Marks : 40

Number of Questions : 40

Time : 2 Hours

There is no negative marking in the test.

Section I

Word and Structure Knowledge

DIRECTIONS (Qs. 1 to 4): Choose the odd one out from each set of words.

1. (a) Doctor   (b) Teacher

   (c) Plumber   (d) Student

2. (a) Telephone   (b) Letter

   (c) Television   (d) Computer

3. (a) Kangaroo   (b) Leopard

   (c) Horse   (d) Frog

4. (a) Ladies : Gentlemen

   (b) Salt : Pepper

   (c) Fruits: Vegetables

   (d) Bread: Cheese

DIRECTIONS (Qs. 5 to 7): Choose the correct spelling.

5. (a) Waelthy   (b) Wealthi

   (c) Wealthy   (d) Wealthe

6. (a) Anethor   (b) Another

   (c) Anather   (d) Anuthuer

7. (a) Breathe   (b) Braethe

   (c) Breethe   (d) Breethe

———— Space for Rough Work ————

DIRECTIONS (Qs. 8 to 21): Fill in the blanks with the most suitable word.

8. The ______ are related to dogs and foxes.

   (a) kittens   (b) wolves

   (c) cubs   (d) puppies

9. He is happy playing with his friends but______ when he's studying.

   (a) sad   (b) pretty

   (c) noisy   (d) short

10. Carry your woollens to Shimla as it would be______ there.

    (a) chill   (b) cold

    (c) colder   (d) spring

11. I come between Friday and Sunday. I am _____.

    (a) Monday   (b) Tuesday

    (c) Saturday   (d) Wednesday

12. The hare ran _____ than the tortoise.

    (a) fast   (b) faster

    (c) fastest   (d) slow

13. This is my ball. I will not give ___ to you.

    (a) him   (b) her

    (c) it   (d) the

14. I saw _____ sunset.

    (a) the   (b) an

    (c) a   (d) it

15. The birds make their nests ___ trees.

    (a) on   (b) in

    (c) at   (d) near

———— Space for Rough Work ————

16. There _____ a girl sitting on that bench.

    (a) is

    (b) are

    (c) am

    (d) none of these

17. I go to school ___7:30 everyday.

    (a) in   (b) on

    (c) the   (d) at

18. The girl is _____ in the sand.

    (a) running   (b) playing

    (c) watching   (d) sleeping

19. The dog is hiding ___ the door.

    (a) near   (b) behind

    (c) beside   (d) at

20. You cannot enter ___ you are late.

    (a) while   (b) because

    (c) when   (d) so

21. Sheena has to ___ the rules, if she has to enter the palace.

    (a) keep   (b) break

    (c) make   (d) place

Section II

Reading

DIRECTIONS (Qs. 22 to 25): Read the passage and choose the best answer to complete the sentences.

Mrs. Paula was very fond of gardening. She used to take care of her garden as her own baby. She always watered her plants daily. Her garden was very beautiful. It had become the talk of the town. It had a vast variety of flowers. It was a colourful sight. Mrs. Paula was also very proud of her garden. But one day she noticed that the leaves of some plants were infected. She didn't know what to do? One of her friends suggested her to use pesticides to get rid of the pests. She could not agree on that. She thought that this way her plants will become poisonous too! So she went to another friend of hers and he suggested her to use herbicides. She did the same and was able to get rid of the infection without causing harm to the environment.

———————— Space for Rough Work ————————

22. Mrs. Paula was fond of __________.

    (a) gardening

    (b) making garlands

    (c) watering plants

    (d) shopping

23. One day she noticed that ______________.

    (a) her plants were infected.

    (b) her plants had grown enormously.

    (c) there were insects in her plants.

    (d) the garden had vanished.

24. She disagreed on using pesticides because______________.

    (a) they were expensive.

    (b) they were not easily available.

    (c) they would make the plants poisonous.

    (d) she had already tried them.

25. Synonym of vast is

    (a) Small   (b) Little

    (c) Kind   (d) Huge

DIRECTIONS (Qs. 26 to 29): Read the letter and choose the best answer to complete the sentences that follow.

Dear Sam,

Hope you are in good health. I am also in good health here. I came to know that you have topped in your school. Congratulations!

I know you are really good in your studies. Studies are an important aspect of our life. But taking care of your health is equally important. We need to do a little bit of physical activity to stay fit. During the breaks, you can always go for a short walk. If you don't like walking, you can dance or play a game of your choice. Remember these things must involve body movements.

Hope you will understand my comments as a genuine concern and not as criticism to put you down.

Hope to see you coming Sunday. Till then bye.

Yours,

Danny

26. This letter is written to _______.

    (a) a friend   (b) a boss

    (c) a neighbour   (d) a son

27. Sam is very good in_________.

    (a) sports   (b) studies

    (c) exercise   (d) drawing

28. Danny is suggesting Sam to _________.

    (a) concentrate on studies

    (b) do exercise

    (c) better his drawing

    (d) behave properly

29. We must pay as much attention to studies as to _________.

    (a) physical activities

    (b) handwriting

    (c) drawing

    (d) attendance in school

Section III

Spoken and Written Expression

DIRECTIONS (Qs. 30 to 35): Choose the best answer to complete the conversation.

30. Meena: Have you read this book?

    Sheena:______________

    (a) Why will I?

    (b) No, I haven't.

    (c) Is this your book?

    (d) This book is mine.

31. Rahul: I forgot to bring my pens. Can you please give me one pen?

    Nazia: ________________________

    (a) Yes, sure.

    (b) No, they are my pens.

    (c) Why should I give it to you?

    (d) Are you silly?

32. Hello, my name is Dev. What's your name?

    Akshat: ________________________

    (a) It's so funny.

    (b) I am Akshat.

    (c) Your name is too short.

    (d) I don't know.

33. Cindy: Can you please tell me the answer of this question?

    Laura: ________________________

    (a) It has no answer.

    (b) I don't know.

    (c) Yes, sure.

    (d) You are very lazy.

34. Krish: I went to the zoo yesterday.

    Shyam: ________________________

    (a) Great! What did you see there?

    (b) I will come with you.

    (c) I was very busy yesterday.

    (d) Which forest?

35. Aryan: Is this your bag?

    Kashish: ________________________

    (a) Yes, it's mine.

    (b) Yes, it's yours.

    (c) Yes, I wanted to take it.

    (d) But who told you?

Section IV

Achievers Section

DIRECTIONS (Qs. 36 to 40): Choose the sentence which should follow the given sentence.

36. He is going to his office.

    ____

    (a) He will reach his office at 9:30 a.m.
    (b) His boss is Mr. Sharma.
    (c) He has a cabin there.
    (d) It's raining outside.

37. Bankeylal is a postman.

    ____

    (a) He works in a school.
    (b) He delivers letters.
    (c) He catches thieves.
    (d) He loves to see burgers.

38. Waiter: Good afternoon! What can I get for you?

    ____

    (a) Some starters, please!
    (b) Is it a hotel?
    (c) What do you like?
    (d) I don't know.

39. We should plant trees to protect our earth _____________________.

    (a) otherwise the animals will run away.
    (b) otherwise our earth will be destroyed.
    (c) otherwise we will not have enough food.
    (d) otherwise our earth will get polluted.

40. We should always check the expiry of the things we buy.

    ____

    (a) We might use expired things and fall sick.
    (b) We might fall down.
    (c) We might smell bad.
    (d) We might start running.

———— Space for Rough Work ————

OLYMPIAD
Mock Test 2

Name : ___________

Number of Questions : 35

Max. Marks : 35

Time : 2 Hours

There is no negative marking in the test.

Section I

Word and Structure Knowledge

DIRECTIONS (Qs. 1 to 4): Pick the odd word.

1. (a) Cucumber   (b) Banana

   (c) Muskmelon   (d) Apple

2. (a) Square   (b) Triangle

   (c) Circle   (d) Rectangle

3. (a) Bread   (b) Knife

   (c) Muffins   (d) Cake

4. (a) Bark   (b) Roar

   (c) Howl   (d) Sing

DIRECTIONS (Qs. 5 to 7): Form meaningful sentences.

5. Go and play__________.

   (a) football

   (b) ballfoot

   (c) bollfat

   (d) talfbol

6. I am mostly black in colour. I grow on your head.

   I am _______.

   (a) hair   (b) hiar

   (c) hrai   (d) irah

Space for Rough Work

7. You wear me when you feel cold.

   I am a ____________.

   (a) seawter   (b) sweater

   (c) swaeter   (d) sweetar

DIRECTIONS (Qs. 8 to 16): Choose the most suitable word.

8. You _______ me that you will study.

   (a) help   (b) promised

   (c) borrowed   (d) sure

9. He has ________ that book from the library.

   (a) lent   (b) borrowed

   (c) asked   (d) promised

10. I went to school ______ my friend.

    (a) with   (b) when

    (c) among   (d) few

11. Can you ______ there?

    (a) come   (b) go

    (c) going   (d) goes

12. Shally brought a ______ of flowers.

    (a) branch   (b) dozen

    (c) bench   (d) bouquet

13. The lion ____ to scare the other animals.

    (a) howled   (b) barked

    (c) neighed   (d) roared

14. We must never ______food.

    (a) waist   (b) waste

    (c) wast   (d) west

15. A place near the sea is called a ____________.

    (a) land   (b) beach

    (c) ocean   (d) lake

16. ______ all going to watch the movie.

    (a) They   (b) Their

    (c) There   (d) They're

DIRECTIONS (Qs. 17 to 20): Choose the best answer.

17. We_______waste to make the puppets.
    (a) used   (b) made
    (c) spent   (d) apply

18. When I met him , he seemed to have_______ taller.
    (a) grown   (b) groan
    (c) gone   (d) come

19. __________ studies animals.
    (a) Pianist   (b) Musician
    (c) Florist   (d) Zoologist

20. You will have to put in _________ effort.
    (a) few   (b) no
    (c) more   (d) much

Section II

Reading

DIRECTIONS (Qs. 21 to 24): Read the poem given below and answer the questions.

Queens, princes, and kings

Cannot, Cannot stay without a lot of things,

Be it anyone, queen or a billionaire,

Will you not use a comb to comb your hair?

If you wished to keep yourself clean,

Though I may sound mean,

But I am sure and hope,

That we all will need a soap,

We all need these few things,

Water, air and food.

Be it poor, rich or a king,

No one can eat gold in place of food.

We all take out a pen to write,

A book to read and a paper to write on.

These are the daily things we all need.

21. What are the three things we all need?

   (a) Cake, pizza and burger

   (b) Water, air and food

   (c) Pen, pencil and eraser

   (d) Pollution, medicine and doctor

22. The kings also need____.

   (a) palaces

   (b) air, water and food

   (c) gold and silver

   (d) good clothes

23. When we want to write, we all use______.

   (a) computer   (b) pen

   (c) pencil   (d) mobile

24. We _________ a book.

   (a) write   (b) read

   (c) watch   (d) look

DIRECTIONS (Qs. 25 to 29): Read the passage and select the best answer.

We all were wondering what had gone wrong, when the airhostess asked us to keep calm. Soon we realised that the plane was landing. We were told to get off the plane. As we were getting off the plane, we heard the police sirens. There were a lot of police activities going on. We even saw the bomb disposal squad. We were told that there was a bomb in the plane. We were scared. Later the bomb disposal squad have found the bomb and disposed it off. After about three hours we were were able to fly in the same aircraft.

25. Why was the plane landing?

   (a) The fuel got finished.

   (b) There was defect in the plane.

   (c) The pilot was tired.

   (d) There was a bomb in the plane.

26. What did the passengers see on getting off?

   (a) The scenery of the place

   (b) The other passengers

   (c) The police activity

   (d) The airport

27. What does the bomb disposal squad do?

   (a) It bursts bombs.

   (b) It detects bombs and diffuses them.

   (c) It collects the bombs.

   (d) It plays with them.

28. When the passengers came to know the reason of landing, they were_________.

   (a) happy   (b) anxious

   (c) scared   (d) sad

29. After about _________, we were able to fly.

   (a) One day   (b) Three hours

   (c) One week   (d) One hour

Section III

Spoken and Written Expression

DIRECTIONS (Qs. 30 to 35): Choose the best reply to complete each conversation.

30. Sheena: Hello, Ayan, where had you been?

   Ayan: _________________

   (a) I am here.

   (b) I had gone to Austria.

   (c) I cannot tell you.

   (d) He was out of country.

31. Fred: How's America?

    Harris: _______________

    (a) Japan is beautiful.

    (b) It's a lovely place.

    (c) I don't know.

    (d) He knows it better.

32. Student: When can I meet the Principal?

    Peon: _______________________

    (a) He is free tomorrow after 12:30.

    (b) I have no idea.

    (c) He doesn't want to meet you.

    (d) That's very tough to tell.

33. Ram: Would you like to come for dinner tomorrow?

    Rohit: _______________________

    (a) How can I come?

    (b) Sorry, it's my sister's birthday tomorrow.

    (c) Today is my birthday.

    (d) You can't tell me that.

34. John: I was late for work, I got up very late.

    Steve: _______________________

    (a) Try to get up early.

    (b) That's not good.

    (c) I am late, too.

    (d) He wanted to go with you.

35. Customer: How much for this watch?

    Shopkeeper: _________________

    (a) It's very expensive.

    (b) I cannot sell it.

    (c) Rs. 1000. It shows date and month also.

    (d) You can go to another shop.

<hr>

Space for Rough Work

OLYMPIAD
Mock Test 3

Name : ___________

Number of Questions : 40

Max. Marks : 40

Time : 2 Hours

There is no negative marking in the test.

Section I

Word and Structure Knowledge

DIRECTIONS (Qs. 1 to 4): Pick the odd word.

1. (a) Lion   (b) Tiger

    (c) Leopard   (d) Horse

2. (a) Drum   (b) Guitar

    (c) Synthesiser (d) Musician

3. (a) Mouse   (b) Peacock

    (c) Rabbit   (d) Dog

4. (a) Lunch   (b) Breakfast

    (c) Dinner   (d) Meal

DIRECTIONS (Qs. 5 to 7): Choose the correct spelling.

5. (a) Nsoe   (b) Nose

    (c) Neso   (d) Sone

6. (a) Ebgine   (b) Enbig

    (c) Begin   (d) Bigen

7. (a) Shcool   (b) School

    (c) Scoohl   (d) Scholo

DIRECTIONS (Qs. 8 to 14): Choose the most suitable word.

8. Mr. Ben is a doctor. ________ is a child specialist.

    (a) He   (b) She

    (c) It   (d) Him

Space for Rough Work

9. I have bought _______ aquarium for my house.

(a) a

(b) an

(c) the

(d) none of these

10. I live _______ the seventh floor of the building.

(a) in   (b) on

(c) at   (d) above

11. I love my country India. I have _______ here since birth.

(a) lived   (b) come

(c) survived   (d) living

12. Do you ___ a spare shirt?

(a) have   (b) has

(c) had   (d) having

13. The postman_______ letters in this area.

(a) delivers

(b) send

(c) delivered

(d) brought

14. How much did you _______ for this dress?

(a) paid   (b) pay

(c) paying   (d) will pay

DIRECTIONS (Qs. 15 to 20): Choose the best answer.

15. I wanted to drink some cold drink not _______ tea.

(a) hot   (b) colder

(c) frozen   (d) icy

16. Elephant : _____:: Horse : neighs

    (a) trumpets   (b) roars

    (c) moos   (d) trumpet

17. Food to grow : Exercise to _____ .

    (a) grow more

    (b) become thin

    (c) stay fit

    (d) win races

18. Earth is a planet: Moon is a _____

    (a) star   (b) satellite

    (c) galaxy   (d) planet

19. Seawater is_____________.

    (a) salty   (b) sour

    (c) sweet   (d) bland

20. I want to eat a ____ of cake.

    (a) peace   (b) piece

    (c) peas   (d) peice

Section II

Reading

DIRECTIONS (Qs. 21 to 25): Read the poem and answer the questions.

I am a butterfly,

I have colourful wings,

Blue, black and pink.

Blue is like dipped in ink,

I love to sit on flowers,

The flowers love when I sit on them,

You want to catch me,

But you can't,

I will fly from plant to plant,

God has made me so beautiful,

Among other things

I am a butterfly with colourful wings.

21. This poem talks of a _______.

    (a) flower   (b) butterfly

    (c) bird   (d) insect

———————————— Space for Rough Work ————————————

22. The butterfly has __________ wings.

   (a) red   (b) pink

   (c) colourful   (d) yellow

23. It sits on _______.

   (a) trees   (b) plants

   (c) flowers   (d) rooftop

24. We can't catch it because_______.

   (a) we can't run very fast

   (b) it will fly away

   (c) it has no house

   (d) we don't have a trap

25. According to you, wings of a butterfly are ______.

   (a) rough   (b) smooth

   (c) soft   (d) hard

DIRECTIONS (Qs. 26 to 29): Read the passage given below and select the best answer.

Ken was too scared of swimming. He was worried that he would drown and die while swimming. His sister made fun of him when he told her about his fear. She called him by different names. Ken was annoyed with his sister for laughing at him. He was determined to swim. Ken's sister felt sorry for him. She offered to teach him swimming.

On the day they went to the pool, they realised that it had been a long time that they did things together. They were surprised that they had so much to share. Ken's fear of swimming also went off.

They were quite happy to have spent time together. The two siblings agreed to spend more time together.

26. Ken was scared of _________.

   (a) swimming

   (b) hiking

   (c) cycling

   (d) riding a horse

27. His sister used to__________.

    (a) scare him off

    (b) make fun of him

    (c) take him out

    (d) hit him

28. Ken was scared of going to pool because____________.

    (a) he thought that water will get over

    (b) he thought he will drown

    (c) he thought he will jump

    (d) he thought that he will hurt himself

29. On the day they went to pool, they ___________.

    (a) realised that they had so much to share

(b) realised that road was really bad

(c) realised that pool was broken

(d) realised that swimming was really tough

Section III

Spoken and Written Expression

DIRECTIONS (Qs. 30 to 35): Choose the best reply to complete each conversation.

30. Tom : Can you tell me the time?

    Tim: ____________________

    (a) It's not easy to say.

    (b) It's quarter past nine.

    (c) I have reached there by 6:30.

    (d) Tomorrow I will come and study with you.

———————— Space for Rough Work ————————

31. Yan: What are they doing?

 Yang:_______________

 (a) I don't know. Let's go and see.

 (b) What a funny question!

 (c) How do I know?

 (d) My mom will come anytime.

32. Pam : Have you seen my book? I can't find it.

 Laura: _____________________

 (a) I am not supposed to tell you.

 (b) Did you look for it in your cupboard?

 (c) My book is in my bag.

 (d) I am not a good reader.

33. Asha: When will the movie start?

 Abha: ___________________

 (a) I like watching movies.

 (b) I am not so fond of watching movies.

 (c) At 5:50.

 (d) That's a funny question.

34. Stay away! The pillar is about to fall.

 ____

 (a) How dare you!

 (b) Thanks for saving my life.

 (c) I like to watch falling pillars.

 (d) Sure, I'll reach on time.

35. Vedant: Do you have a hobby?

 Ved: ___________________

 (a) You can't talk to me like this.

 (b) That's my choice.

 (c) Why should I tell you?

 (d) Yes, I love collecting stamps.

———————————— Space for Rough Work ————————————

Section IV

Achievers Section

DIRECTIONS (Qs. 36 to 40): Choose the best option.

36. Can you add a_____ of sugar to the tea?

    (a) pinch   (b) spoon

    (c) few   (d) more

37. He cannot write. He has hurt his thumb.

    (a) He cannot write so he has hurt his thumb.

    (b) He cannot write because he has hurt his thumb

    (c) He cannot write when he has hurt his thumb

    (d) He cannot write while he has hurt his thumb.

38. One sheep, many ________

    (a) sheeps   (b) sheepes

    (c) sheaps   (d) sheep

39. One baby; many ________

    (a) babies   (b) babyies

    (c) babis   (d) babys

40. Poly: I want to learn guitar. What about you?

    Paul:______________

    (a) No, thanks.

    (b) I play very good flute.

    (c) I also want to.

    (d) That's so funny.

OLYMPIAD
Mock Test 4

Name : _____________

Max. Marks : 35

Number of Questions : 35

Time : 2 Hours

There is no negative marking in the test.

Section I

Word and Structure Knowledge

DIRECTIONS (Qs. 1 to 4): Choose the odd one out from each set of words.

1. (a) Bread   (b) Coffee
   (c) Tea   (d) Juice

2. (a) Bike   (b) Bicycle
   (c) Scooter   (d) Car

3. (a) Starfish   (b) Shark
   (c) Whale   (d) Horse

4. (a) Cricket   (b) Football
   (c) Basketball   (d) Chess

DIRECTIONS (Qs. 5 to 7): Choose the correct spelling.

5. (a) Shup   (b) Push
   (c) Upsh   (d) Shpu

6. (a) Hospitel   (b) Hospital
   (c) Haspitol   (d) Hispatol

7. (a) Cheldrin   (b) Children
   (c) Cildhren   (d) Renchild

DIRECTIONS (Qs. 8 to 16): Choose the most suitable word.

8. Fifty comes _____ fifty one.
   (a) before   (b) after
   (c) on   (d) in between

Space for Rough Work

9. Did you _____ the howl of a fox?

   (a) hare   (b) hear

   (c) here   (d) haer

10. Are you ___this book?

   (a) watching   (b) reading

   (c) looking   (d) making

11. His mother makes _______food.

   (a) wow   (b) tasty

   (c) dirty   (d) smooth

12. This cloth is very rough, give me _____cloth.

   (a) soft   (b) smooth

   (c) hard   (d) cotton

13. This is ____ Eucalyptus tree. It gives us many medicines.

   (a) an

   (b) a

   (c) the

   (d) none of these

14. There is so _____ work to do.

   (a) few   (b) much

   (c) no   (d) more

15. Go _____, you will find a shop.

   (a) here   (b) there

   (c) where   (d) nowhere

16. Give me a scoop of ________.

   (a) cake   (b) ice cream

   (c) toffee   (d) chocolate

DIRECTIONS (Qs. 17 to 20): Choose the best answer.

17. Miss Rita is a writer.___ writings are liked by children.

   (a) Their   (b) Her

   (c) She   (d) His

18. It ___ always said no news is good news.

    (a) is   (b) are

    (c) were   (d) was

19. I ___ a very bright student in my school days. I always came first in class.

    (a) am   (b) was

    (c) is   (d) are

20. Every morning I ____ my dog for a walk.

    (a) taken   (b) took

    (c) take   (d) taking

Section II

Reading

DIRECTIONS (Qs. 21 to 25): Read the poem and answer the questions.

Once there was a cute little boy,

But he did not want to be cute,

He wanted to be strong and not coy,

What he loved was to watch movies,

That had strong heroes.

He liked to watch them all day,

Movies that ended with the hero winning,

For that, at home he loved to stay,

But his mom didn't like

his watching movies too much,

She was afraid that movies were such,

That would spoil his brain,

She stopped his movie watching.

What could the boy do?

He gave up his movie watching,

And went to the school.

21. The boy was ______.

    (a) strong

    (b) well-behaved

    (c) cute

    (d) smart

22. The boy wanted to be______________.
    - (a) good in studies
    - (b) strong
    - (c) cute
    - (d) tough

23. He loved ______.
    - (a) playing football
    - (b) watching movies
    - (c) studying
    - (d) eating good food

24. His mother did____________.
    - (a) not like his movie watching
    - (b) like to watch movies with him
    - (c) not want him to study
    - (d) not want him to eat junk food

25. Finally the boy__________.
    - (a) gave up studies
    - (b) went to the school
    - (c) ate all the cake
    - (d) left his games

DIRECTIONS (Qs. 26 to 29): Read the passage and select the best answer.

Dam was a dragon girl. She did not know what to eat. She was quite an unusual dragon because she did not like meat. But she did not like vegetables too! So her mother did not know what to give her. One day, Dam's father went out to look for food. He brought some papayas. Dam was so excited to see the yellow fruit that she gobbled the whole of it. She wanted to have more of it. Dam's mother was so happy that finally Dam was eating something.

26. Dam was a __________.
    - (a) sweet girl
    - (b) dragon girl
    - (c) boy
    - (d) lion

27. What did Dam like to eat?
    - (a) Meat
    - (b) Nothing
    - (c) Vegetables
    - (d) Bread

28. Why did Dam's father go out?

   (a) To look for food

   (b) To collect some water

   (c) To play with his friends

   (d) To buy vegetables

29. What did Dam finally like to eat?

   (a) Sugar   (b) Papaya

   (c) Strawberry   (d) Pizza

Section III

Spoken and Written Expression

DIRECTIONS (Qs. 30 to 35): Choose the best reply to complete each conversation.

30. Meena: This is my uncle Sam. He stays in Africa.

   Sheena: _______________________

   (a) Don't tell me that.

   (b) Nice to meet you.

   (c) Why has he come here?

   (d) This is not my house.

31. Fanny: Please put on the lights. I cannot see anything.

   Sam : _______________________

   (a) Sure.

   (b) Are you blind?

   (c) This is not my job.

   (d) Don't be silly, come.

32. Tom : Ms. Jane, is it your first trip to Mumbai?

   Jane : _______________

   (a) That picture is so beautiful.

   (b) I'll like to have a cup of tea.

   (c) Yes, everything is new to me. Mumbai is lovely.

   (d) What are you saying?

33. Nisha: What time will you go for shopping?

Rita: ______________________

(a) Why should I go?

(b) I don't know anything.

(c) At 7:30.

(d) That's a funny question.

34. Dad: Sonu, why have you broken that glass?

Sonu: ______________________

(a) I am so sorry, it was by mistake.

(b) I haven't.

(c) Someone else did it.

(d) Glass is not too expensive.

35. Doctor: I am giving you a few medicines, take them on time.

Patient: ______________________

(a) How dare you ask me!

(b) Better, thanks for the concern.

(c) Sure, I'll take them.

(d) You never told me that.

Name : __________

Number of Questions : 35

Max. Marks : 35

Time : 2 Hours

There is no negative marking in the test.

Section I
Word and Structure Knowledge

DIRECTIONS (Qs. 1 to 4): Choose the odd one out from each set of words.

1. (a) Shoe   (b) Sandal
   (c) Glove   (d) Boot

2. (a) Rice   (b) Pork
   (c) Chicken   (d) Beef

3. (a) Chair   (b) Desk
   (c) Sofa   (d) Bed

4. (a) Cub   (b) Kitten
   (c) Fish   (d) Puppy

DIRECTIONS (Qs. 5 to 7): Choose the correct spelling.

5. (a) Roomb   (b) Broom
   (c) Roomb   (d) Mobro

6. (a) Neck   (b) Nack
   (c) Neke   (d) Nekc

7. (a) Plaese   (b) Please
   (c) Pleese   (d) Plesae

DIRECTIONS (Qs. 8 to 16): Choose the most suitable word.

8. Manish's parents had gone to school. _______ went by car.
   (a) He   (b) She
   (c) They   (d) Them

9. He saw _____octopus in the river.
   (a) a
   (b) an
   (c) the
   (d) none of these

Space for Rough Work

10. One woman: Many _____

    (a) Womens   (b) Womans

    (c) Women   (d) Woman

11. Goat bleats : Crow__________

    (a) Pipes   (b) Sings

    (c) Croaks   (d) Roars

12. If light is to summer, then dark is to_____.

    (a) winter   (b) spring

    (c) autumn   (d) monsoon

13. The monkey is jumping ___ the tree.

    (a) at   (b) in

    (c) on   (d) over

14. You go and _____peace with him.

    (a) break   (b) place

    (c) take   (d) make

15. My friend stays in Australia. She _____ two children.

    (a) has   (b) had

    (c) have   (d) will have

16. I have won the trophy. I ____very fast.

    (a) run   (b) ran

    (c) will run   (d) running

DIRECTIONS (Qs. 17 to 20): Choose the best answer.

17. He will not be able to attend the concert. He is not there in town.

    (a) He will not be able to attend the concert because he is not there in town.

    (b) He will not be able to attend the concert so he is not there on town.

    (c) He will not be able to attend the concert while he is not there in town.

    (d) He will not be able to attend after he is not there in the town.

18. Earth revolves around ____ Sun.

    (a) a   (b) an

    (c) the   (d) at

19. I want to gift you this doll. Now it is ___________.

   (a) mine   (b) yours

   (c) ours   (d) us

20. _____ is the principal's son? Have you met him?

   (a) Who   (b) What

   (c) Which   (d) How

Section II

Reading

DIRECTIONS (Qs. 21 to 25): Read the passage and answer the following questions.

Once upon a time, there was a king. He was very fond of listening to praises. He did not know that the ones who were praising him were not doing so genuinely. He had only one son who was just twelve years old. His son kept on telling him about it. But the king did not believe his son. So his son thought of a plan.

Next day he asked his ministers, "Who is the wisest king?"

'Your Majesty', said his ministers, "You are the wisest king in the world".

'Ah'! The king was very happy and gave gold coins to each of his ministers.

There was one minister who sat in the corner and did not say anything.

The king went to him and asked "don't you agree with what the other ministers have said?"

The minister got up and said "your Majesty, my answer would be different from the rest of the ministers. I am afraid you may not like it". The king assured him safety of life. The minister said, "You are a wise King, but there have been kings wiser than you".

The king was amazed at his truthfulness, he wanted to put him in prison. But he had already promised him safety of life.

His son advised him to appoint that minister as his chief adviser. The king listened to his son and did the same.

21. The king was fond of________.

   (a) wandering around

   (b) listening to praises

   (c) buying new clothes

   (d) selling crafts

22. His son ___________.

   (a) knew that all praises were false

   (b) also wanted to become the king

   (c) wanted his father to play with him

   (d) wanted to go for horse riding

23. The king asked his ministers ________.

   (a) about the wisest king in the world

   (b) about the most handsome person in this world

   (c) about the most healthy person in this world

   (d) about the most happy person in this world

24. One minister sat quietly because ________.

   (a) he did not agree with the other ministers

   (b) he did not want to answer

   (c) he was unable to speak

   (d) he was scared of speaking the truth

25. Why didn't the king put that minister into prison?

   (a) There was shortage of prisons.

   (b) There were no prisons.

   (c) He had promised him safety of life.

   (d) He was scared of attack by enemy.

DIRECTIONS (Qs. 26 to 29): Read the poem and select the best answer.

I went to the zoo and met a monkey,

It swung around a lot and looked very funky,

Then I saw a big brown bear,

It looked very big and had a lot of hair,

I saw a lion in a den,

It roared louder than fifty men,

The zoo is such a fun place to be,

Let's go back there, and see.

26. Where did the author go?

    (a) To the zoo

    (b) To the jungle

    (c) To the museum

    (d) To a park

27. He saw a monkey______.

    (a) swinging here and there.

    (b) eating bananas

    (c) riding a bicycle

    (d) snatching caps from people

28. He saw a bear; it was too ________.

    (a) small   (b) big

    (c) kind   (d) happy

29. The lion was in its _____.

    (a) kennel   (b) den

    (c) shed   (d) nest

Section III

Spoken and Written Expressions

DIRECTIONS (Qs. 30 to 35): Choose the best reply to complete each conversation.

30. Rohan: Did you live in tents?

    Rohit:_______________________

    (a) Yes, we did.

    (b) That's my tent.

    (c) That was not required.

    (d) Our coach did not let us go out in open.

31. Mr Glenn: Who cooks food for you?

    Mr. James: ___________

    (a) I don't eat food.

    (b) I cook my own food.

    (c) I drink water.

    (d) That's a silly question.

32. Amit: Why are trees so tall in Kerela?

    Sumit: ___________________

    (a) That's because Kerela gets a lot of rain.

    (b) That's because we stretch them.

    (c) They are not so tall, I am taller.

    (d) It sounds so funny.

33. Sharon: Whose picture is this?

    Shan: ___________________

    (a) I don't know.

    (b) It is mine.

    (c) I cannot say.

    (d) It seems to be raining.

34. Steve: Whose white car is that?

    Deb: _______________________

    (a) That is broken.

    (b) It belongs to my friend.

    (c) Why do you want to know?

    (d) Is it yours?

35. Tim: Let's go to the museum today.

    Sim: _________________

    (a) I don't have time.

    (b) Sure, what time?

    (c) I can't tell you.

    (d) That's a tough question.

MATHEMATICS MOCK TEST 1-5

Name : _____________

Number of Questions : 35

Max. Marks : 35

Time : 2 Hours

There is no negative marking in the test.

1. Which of the following is a true statement?

   (a) $\boxed{89}$ has $\boxed{8}$ tens
   (b) $\boxed{78}$ has $\boxed{6}$ tens
   (c) $\boxed{56}$ has $\boxed{5}$ ones
   (d) $\boxed{26}$ has $\boxed{6}$ tens

2. The digit at the place of tens in 812 is _____________.

   (a) 8
   (b) 2
   (c) 1
   (d) 6

3. Place value of 3 in 239 is

   (a) 300
   (b) 3
   (c) 30
   (d) 3000

4. Which of the following roll and slide?

   (a) Football
   (b) Book
   (c) Glass
   (d) Orange

5. Add the number given in the triangle.

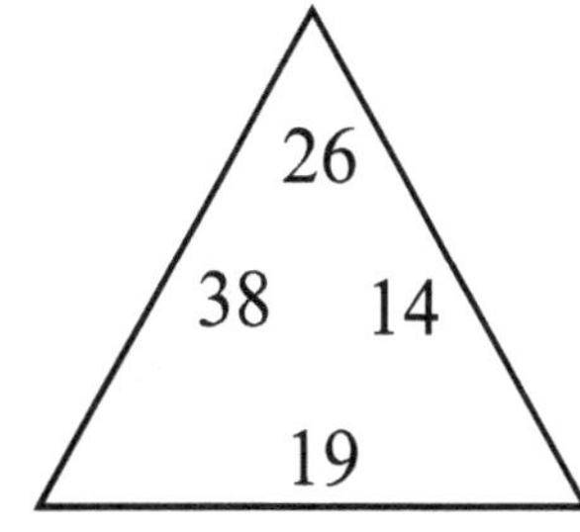

   (a) 98
   (b) 97
   (c) 79
   (d) 76

6. Add the following.

   (a) 97
   (b) 78
   (c) 99
   (d) 70

Space for Rough Work

7. Sakshi bought 14 mangoes, 12 apples, 1 watermelon and 6 bananas. How many fruits did she buy in all?

   (a) 38　　　　　(b) 29

   (c) 30　　　　　(d) 33

8. There are 25 people sitting in a garden. After sometime, 128 more people come into the park. How many people are there in the park now?

   (a) 129　　　　(b) 145

   (c) 148　　　　(d) 153

9. There are 520 students in a school. Out of which, 38 students were absent on Thursday. How many students were present on Thursday?

   (a) 482　　　　(b) 484

   (c) 486　　　　(d) 488

10. Shalvi buys 624 eggs from the market. Later on, she finds that 15 of them were rotten. How many eggs were in good condition?

   (a) 605　　　　(b) 506

   (c) 517　　　　(d) 609

11. A week has 7 days. How many days will be there in 4 weeks?

   (a) 14　　　　　(b) 21

   (c) 28　　　　　(d) 30

12. What number should be multiplied with 9 to get the result 54?

   (a) 5　　　　　(b) 6

   (c) 7　　　　　(d) 8

13. There are 112 ice creams. These ice creams should be equally divided among 7 girls. How many ice creams will each girl get?

   (a) 15　　　　　(b) 16

   (c) 17　　　　　(d) 18

14. What will be the quotient, if we divide 86 by 2?

   (a) 43　　　　　(b) 42

   (c) 41　　　　　(d) 44

15. Manish brought 36 m tape and used 23 m of it in making a project. How much tape is left?

   (a) 13 m　　　　(b) 12 m

   (c) 8 m　　　　　(d) 10 m

Space for Rough Work

16. Any number subtracted by zero, gives ______.

    (a) 0

    (b) 1

    (c) number itself

    (d) none of these

17. A shopkeeper has 10 bags of rice, each having a weight of 5 kg. What will be the total weight of the rice bags?

    (a) 50 kg   (b) 10 kg

    (c) 500 kg   (d) 20 kg

18. What is the time shown by the following clock?

    (a) 6:15   (b) 4:30

    (c) 3:30   (d) 6:20

19. The month that comes after September is ______.

    (a) July   (b) June

    (c) October   (d) August

20. Match the objects given in column -I with the name of shapes given in column –II.

Column –I		Column –II
(A) 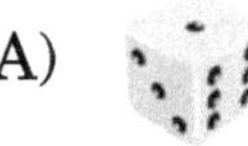		(1) Cone
(B) 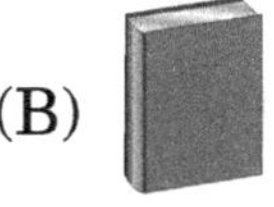		(2) Cylinder
(C) 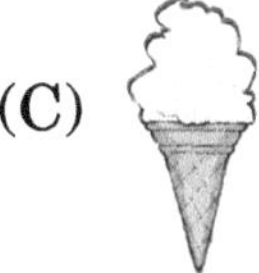		(3) Cube
(D)		(4) Cuboid

	A	B	C	D
(a)	2	4	1	3
(b)	3	4	1	2
(c)	2	1	3	4
(d)	3	1	4	2

DIRECTIONS (Qs. 21 and 22): Use the calendar to answer each of the following questions.

September 2007

Sunday	Monday	Tuesday	Wednesday	Thrusday	Friday	Saturday
			1	2	3	4
5	6	7	8	9	10	11
12	13	14	15	16	17	18
19	20	21	22	23	24	25
26	27	28	29	30		

21. How many days are there in the month of September?

    (a) 30   (b) 31

    (c) 28   (d) 29

22. What is the day on the 28th of September?

    (a) Monday   (b) Tuesday

    (c) Wednesday   (d) Thursday

23. What fraction of the given shape is shaded?

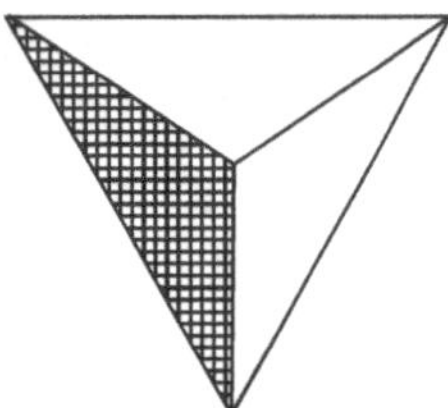

    (a) 1/3   (b) 1/2

    (c) 2/3   (d) 1

24. What fraction of the given shape is unshaded?

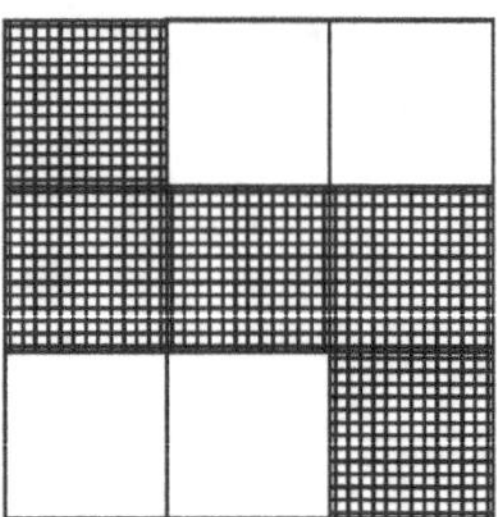

    (a) 5/9   (b) 4/9

    (c) 4/5   (d) 5

25. 40 sweets were packed into 4 bags equally. If each bag had 3 red sweets, how many non-red sweets were there altogether?

    (a) 38   (b) 28

    (c) 30   (d) 40

26. The figure shown below is made up of _____ squares.

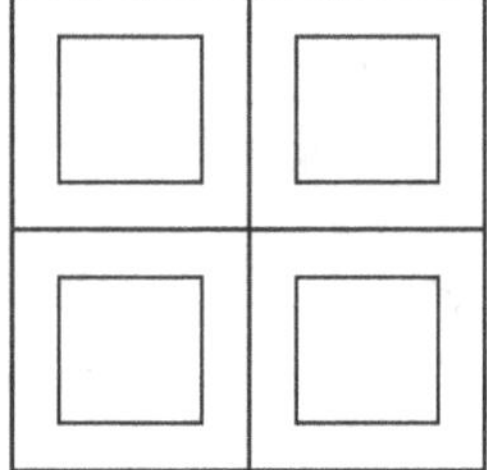

—————————— *Space for Rough Work* ——————————

(a) 18 (b) 20

(c) 9 (d) 30

27. Alia bought a bag for ₹235 and a pair of shoes for ₹362. How much total amount she spent altogether?

(a) ₹636 (b) ₹638

(c) ₹540 (d) ₹597

28. What comes next in the pattern?

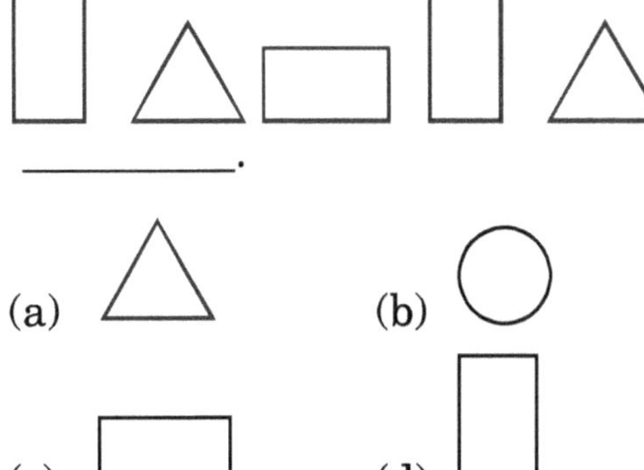

(a) (b)

(c) (d)

29. Complete the following:

32, 30, 28, 26, _______

(a) 25 (b) 24

(c) 22 (d) 23

30. Which of the following completes the figure?

(a) (b)

(c) (d)

31. The height of a tree A is 6 metres and tree B is 3 metres taller than tree A. What will be the height of tree B ?

(a) 6 metres (b) 3 metres

(c) 9 metres (d) 10 metres

32. Aditi purchased 8 kg of mangoes, she gave 4 kg to her friend Sudhi. How much mangoes are left with her?

(a) 2 kg (b) 3 kg

(c) 4 kg (d) 1.5 kg

DIRECTIONS (Qs. 33 to 35) : The table shows the number of boys and girls of class 2 who have birthdays in each month of the year.

S. No.	Month	Girls	Boys
1	January	2	3
2	February	4	3
3	March	1	2
4	April	2	2

———— Space for Rough Work ————

5	May	1	2
6	June	4	0
7	July	8	6
8	August	5	2
9	September	6	1
10	October	3	2
11	November	1	3
12	December	2	1

33. How many boys celebrated their birthdays in the month of June?

(a) 0   (b) 1

(c) 2   (d) 4

34. Which month has the most number of birthdays?

(a) November   (b) June

(c) July   (d) February

35. How many total number of students are there in class 2?

(a) 40   (b) 50

(c) 60   (d) 66

Space for Rough Work

OLYMPIAD
Mock Test 2

1. My uncle bought 60 chocolates and distributed them among Nikky, Raja, Rani, Sachin and Kiran equally. How many chocolates did each child get?

   (a) 10   (b) 12

   (c) 16   (d) 18

2. The sum of numbers from 1 to 10 is __________

   (a) 41   (b) 40

   (c) 48   (d) 55

3. Rohan has eight hundred ninety seven coins with him. How would he write it in numbers ?

   (a) 867   (b) 868

   (c) 879   (d) 897

4. There are 7 pens in each of 9 pen stands. How many total pens are there in all ?

   (a) 63   (b) 64

   (c) 65   (d) 66

5. Ritu reads 24 pages of a book in 12 days. How many pages does she read in 1 day ?

   (a) 2   (b) 4

   (c) 5   (d) 6

6. The number 843 has __________ hundreds.

   (a) 15   (b) 12

   (c) 8   (d) 6

Space for Rough Work

7. Nisha brought a dress worth ₹560 and a hand bag for ₹175. She had given ₹1000 to the shopkeeper. How much money did the shopkeeper return to Nisha ?

   (a) ₹200   (b) ₹265

   (c) ₹300   (d) ₹295

8. 'A' travels a distance of 56 km and 'B' travels a distance of 48 km. Who travels longer distance and by how much?

   (a) 'A' by 8 km   (b) 'B' by 8 km

   (c) 'B' by 12 km   (d) 'B' by 20 km

9. 25 less than 50 is

   (a) 15   (b) 25

   (c) 75   (d) 30

10. Which of the following is not a flat shape?

   (a) 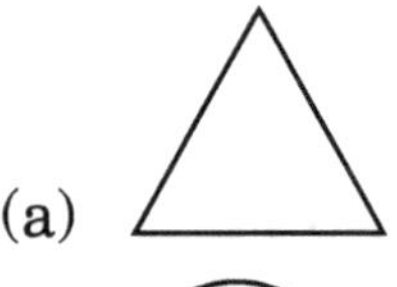   (b)

   (c)    (d)

11. In a cricket match, Rahul scored 126 runs and Sourav scored 98 runs. How many runs did they make altogether?

   (a) 200   (b) 185

   (c) 193   (d) 224

12. There are 64 mangoes in a box. How many mangoes will be there in 5 such boxes?

   (a) 320   (b) 360

   (c) 300   (d) 380

13. Avleen bought a book for ₹125. She gave 2 notes of ₹100. How much amount will the shopkeeper return to Avleen?

   (a) ₹100   (b) ₹90

   (c) ₹75   (d) ₹25

14. In a garden, there are 85 apple trees, 152 banana trees and 125 guava trees. How many total number of trees are present in the garden?

   (a) 362   (b) 350

   (c) 368   (d) 355

Space for Rough Work

15. Which of the following is an odd number?

    (a) 48   (b) 14

    (c) 20   (d) 37

16. In a leap year, Ronnie goes to school 288 days. Find the number of days he did not go to school.

    (a) 45 days   (b) 65 days

    (c) 78 days   (d) 88 days

17. 1 hundred +2 tens + 3 ones is equal to

    (a) 124   (b) 123

    (c) 122   (d) 128

18. Each cup can hold 50 ml of water. What amount of water a jug can hold ?

    (a) 500 ml   (b) 200 ml

    (c) 700 ml   (d) 600 ml

19. What number comes before 300?

    (a) 301   (b) 302

    (c) 299   (d) 401

20. Match the objects with their appropriate unit columns.

    Column – I   **Column – II**

    (A) 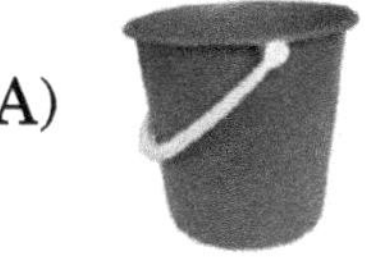   (1) Gram

    (B)    (2) Kilogram

    (C)   (3) Litre

    (D)   (4) Millilitre

	A	B	C	D
(a)	3	4	1	2
(b)	2	4	1	3
(c)	3	1	4	2
(d)	2	1	4	3

--- *Space for Rough Work* ---

21. Find the place value of 9 in 9̲74 .

   (a) 900   (b) 90

   (c) 09   (d) 70

22. What is the time shown by the clock ?

   (a) 7 : 00   (b) 7 : 15

   (c) 8 : 00   (d) 8 : 25

23. Write 796 in words.

   (a) Seven ninety six

   (b) Seven hundred ninety

   (c) Seven hundred ninety and sixty

   (d) Seven hundred and ninety six

24. Which of the following 2 consecutive months have 31 days ?

   (a) January and Febuary

   (b) May and June

   (c) July and August

   (d) March and April

25. A number multplied by 1 gives

   (a) 1   (b) 0

   (c) Number itself (d) 2

26. Which of the following is incorrectly matched ?

   (a) Nine hundred and twenty six = 926

   (b) Two hundred and fifty nine = 2059

   (c) One hundred and ninety = 190

   (d) Two hundred and ninety six = 296

27. Find the odd one out.

   (a) 340, 341, 342

   (b) 461, 462, 463

   (c) 481, 581, 681

   (d) 501, 502, 503

28. Which of the following set of numbers is arranged in increasing order ?

   (a) 571, 597, 578, 587

   (b) 597, 699, 695, 587

   (c) 233, 589, 680, 780

   (d) 281, 259, 355, 456

Space for Rough Work

29. Sana cuts a birthday cake into 9 equal pieces. She distributed 4 pieces to her friends. What fraction of the cake she distributed to her friends ?

(a) $\dfrac{4}{9}$ (b) $\dfrac{3}{9}$

(c) $\dfrac{2}{9}$ (d) $\dfrac{5}{9}$

30. Which fraction of the figure is not shaded ?

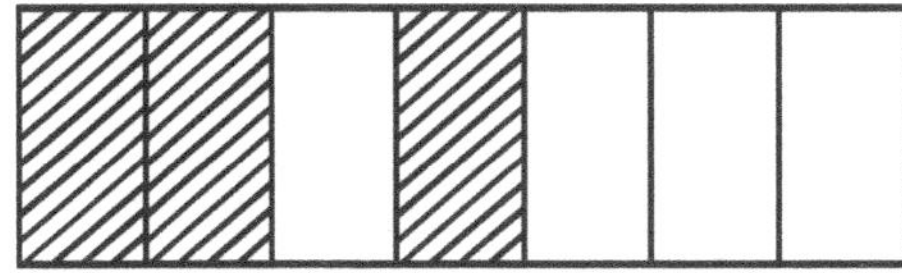

(a) $\dfrac{3}{5}$ (b) $\dfrac{3}{7}$

(c) $\dfrac{4}{7}$ (d) $\dfrac{5}{7}$

31. Complete the pattern.

(a)   (b)

(c)   (d)

32. Complete the pettern.

55, 50, 45, 40, ...

(a) 30   (b) 35

(c) 20   (d) 25

DIRECTIONS (Qs. 33 to 35) : My mother is going to purchase some household products. She makes the list of things she needs to buy.

List of product	Products
1. Tooth paste	1
2. Biscuit	5
3. Maggi	2
4. Coconut chips	3

33. How many packet of biscuits has she purchased ?

(a) 5   (b) 4

(c) 3   (d) 4

34. How many total quantity of products she purchased ?

(a) 11   (b) 10

(c) 9   (d) 8

35. What has been purchased in maximum quantity?

(a) Coconut   (b) Biscuit

(c) Maggi   (d) Toothpaste

OLYMPIAD
Mock Test 3

Name : __________
Number of Questions : 40

Max. Marks : 40
Time : 2 Hours

There is no negative marking in the test.

1. Write the following numbers in short form.

   5 tens + 4 ones = ______

   (a) 50
   (b) 90
   (c) 54
   (d) 60

2. Arrange the given numbers in ascending order.

   | 29, 43, 40, 57, 63 |

   (a) 29, 40, 43, 63, 57
   (b) 29, 40, 43, 57, 63
   (c) 29, 43, 40, 63, 57
   (d) 29, 51, 53, 40, 43

3. Snita scored 48 marks in her first class test and 42 marks in her second class test. How much did she scored in both the test ?

   (a) 90
   (b) 80
   (c) 60
   (d) 50

4. Match the following.

	Column (I)	Column (II)
A.	4×7	1. 0
B.	3×1	2. 2×5
C.	5×2	3. $2 \times 2 \times 7$
D.	0×2	4. 3

	A	B	C	D
(a)	2	3	1	4
(b)	4	3	1	2
(c)	3	4	2	1
(d)	1	4	3	2

5. Ravi has 150 marbles and Sudhi has 132 marbles. How many more marbles does Ravi has than Sudhi ?

─── *Space for Rough Work* ───

(a) 16   (b) 18

(c) 19   (d) 20

6. Which of the following shows the fraction of $\frac{1}{3}$ shaded ?

(a) 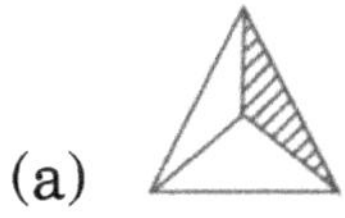   (b) 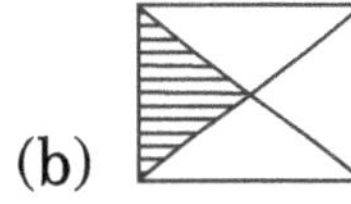

(c) 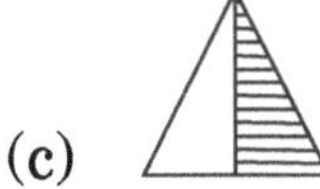   (d) 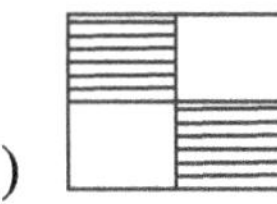

7. Kritika draw a circle and divided the circle into 6 equal parts, coloured 2 parts green, 1 part blue and 1 part red. What will be the fraction of uncoloured part ?

(a) $\frac{2}{6}$ (b) $\frac{3}{6}$

(c) $\frac{1}{6}$ (d) $\frac{4}{6}$

DIRECTIONS (Qs. 8 & 9): The cost of each item is given below.

Ball
₹ 60

Book
₹ 100

Pencil Box
₹ 50

Eraser
₹ 10

8. What is the most expensive item?

(a) Ball

(b) Book

(c) Pencil box

(d) Eraser

9. If Ravi has ₹15, which of the following things can he buy ?

(a) Eraser   (b) Pencil Box

(c) Book   (d) Ball

10. Radha has 10 chocolates, Reena has 6 chocolates more than Radha and Beena has 4 chocolates less than Reena. How many chocolates does Beena have ?

(a) 20

(b) 12

(c) 10

(d) 16

Space for Rough Work

DIRECTIONS (Qs. 11 to 13): The table shows the number of burgers sold from Monday to Friday. Study the table and answer the following question.

Days	No. of burger sold
Monday	4
Tuesday	5
Wednesday	8
Thursday	6
Friday	4

11. On which day, maximum number of burgers sold ?

    (a) Wednesday (b) Monday

    (c) Tuesday (d) Monday

12. On which day, 6 burgers were sold ?

    (a) Monday (b) Wednesday

    (c) Friday (d) Thursday

13. On which days, sale of burgers was same?

    (a) Monday, Tuesday

    (b) Wednesday, Friday

    (c) Monday, Friday

    (d) Tuesday, Thursday

14. Complete the pattern.

    13, 23, 33, 43 _______.

    (a) 47 (b) 63

    (c) 53 (d) 37

15. What will be the quotient if dividend is 56 and divisor is 8?

    (a) 8 (b) 7

    (c) 10 (d) 9

16. What time does the clock show ?

    (a) 2 : 45 (b) 1 : 55

    (c) 7 : 00 (d) 6 : 15

17. How many sides does a square has?

    (a) 4 (b) 3

    (c) 5 (d) 6

18. Complete the following series.

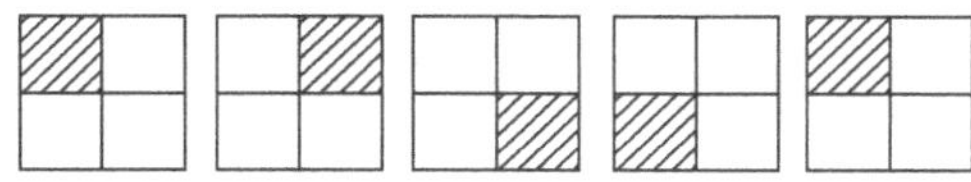

(a)   (b)   (c)   (d)

19. Sara went to the market. She bought vegetables for ₹340. She gave ₹500 to the shopkeeper. How much money will the shopkeeper return to Sara ?

(a) ₹240   (b) ₹260

(c) ₹160   (d) ₹340

20. In a factory, 113 ice creams are produced everyday. How many ice creams does it produce in a week?

(a) 226   (b) 791

(c) 773   (d) 771

21. Which of the following is correct ?

(a) $430 > 421$

(b) $221 > 228$

(c) $330 < 321$

(d) $230 = 320$

22. If today is Tuesday, the day after tomorrow is

(a) Wednesday   (b) Thursday

(c) Monday   (d) Sunday

23. If 660 chairs are arranged in 10 equal rows, then find the total number of chairs in each row ?

(a) 55   (b) 60

(c) 50   (d) 66

24. I am third from left but sixth from the right in the queue. How many people are there in the queue?

(a) 3   (b) 8

(c) 9   (d) 10

25. Choose odd one out.

(a)   (b)   (c)   (d)

26. Which of the following is a 3-D shape ?

    (a) Square   (b) Rectangle

    (c) Circle   (d) Cone

27. Which is the greatest number in the following given numbers?

    (a) 443   (b) 434

    (c) 454   (d) 445

28. The expanded form of 798 is _______.

    (a) 700 + 98   (b) 7 + 9 + 8

    (c) 700+ 90 + 8   (d) 79 + 8

29. Jitesh went to dance class at 10:00 am. and came back at 11:00 am. What is the duration of his class ?

    (a) 1 hour   (b) 2 hours

    (c) 3 hours   (d) 4 hour

30. In number 43, the digit at one's place is

    (a) 4   (b) 2

    (c) 1   (d) 3

31. Complete the pattern.

    (A1) (B2) (C3) (D4) ◯

    (a) E6   (b) F5

    (c) E5   (d) F6

32. In a class, there are 60 students. The number of girls is 10 more than 25. Find the number of boys.

    (a) 35   (b) 36

    (c) 25   (d) 26

33. The capacity of a jug is 16 glasses. How many glasses do we need to fill a jug completely with water?

    (a) 10   (b) 15

    (c) 12   (d) 16

34. 1 hour = ☐ minutes

    (a) 30 minutes

    (b) 100 minutes

    (c) 60 minutes

    (d) 20 minutes

Space for Rough Work

35. Which of the following are in decreasing order ?

    (a) 74, 95, 47, 59

    (b) 59, 47, 95, 74

    (c) 47, 59, 74, 45

    (d) 95, 74, 59, 47

36. An ice cream factory produces 20 ice creams in a day. How many ice creams will it produce in a week if Saturday is holiday ?

    (a) 100

    (b) 120

    (c) 160

    (d) 180

37. If ₹105 is to be divided among 5 persons equally, how much amount will each person get ?

    (a) ₹26

    (b) ₹22

    (c) ₹21

    (d) ₹25

38. Which of the options is correct ?

    (a) $298 < 140$

    (b) $196 < 103$

    (c) $658 < 829$

    (d) $195 < 96$

39. Multiply 85 by 8. What will be the answer ?

    (a) $700 + 10 + 8$

    (b) $700 + 80$

    (c) $600 + 80 + 8$

    (d) $600 + 80$

40. A bag of sugar weighs 23 kg and a bag of rice weighs 25 kg. What will be their total weight.

    (a) 45 kg

    (b) 32 kg

    (c) 48 kg

    (d) 18 kg

Space for Rough Work

OLYMPIAD
Mock Test 4

Name : ___________

Number of Questions : 35

Max. Marks : 35

Time : 2 Hours

There is no negative marking in the test.

1. Which one of the following numbers should be added to 13 to get 26 ?

   (a) 10   (b) 8

   (c) 12   (d) 13

2. How many tens and ones are there in 85 ?

   (a) 9 tens + 8 ones

   (b) 5 tens + 8 ones

   (c) 5 tens + 5 ones

   (d) 8 tens + 5 ones

3. How many sides are there in a triangle ?

   (a) 1   (b) 2

   (c) 3   (d) 4

4. What is the time shown in the clock ?

   (a) 6 : 45   (b) 2 : 10

   (c) 1 : 50   (d) 4 : 30

5. Arup reads 60 pages of a book in a week. How many pages does he read in one day, if he doesn't read book on Saturday ?

   (a) 2   (b) 10

   (c) 5   (d) 6

———— Space for Rough Work ————

6. 1 hour = 60 minutes, 5 hours is equal to ___
   - (a) 110 minutes
   - (b) 300 minutes
   - (c) 10 minutes
   - (d) 200 minutes

7. One bag contains 5 kg of wheat. How much wheat does 10 wheat bags contain ?
   - (a) 300 kg
   - (b) 200 kg
   - (c) 50 kg
   - (d) 400 kg

8. How many days are there in 4 weeks ?
   - (a) 13 days
   - (b) 72 days
   - (c) 28 days
   - (d) 74 days

9. What is the place value of 6 in 672 ?
   - (a) 600
   - (b) 06
   - (c) 6
   - (d) 60

10. A spider has 8 legs. How many legs will 3 spiders have ?
    - (a) 16 legs
    - (b) 32 legs
    - (c) 48 legs
    - (d) 24 legs

11. Nishi bought 457 chocolates on her birthday. She distributed 305 chocolates among his friends. How many chocolates is left with Nishi?
    - (a) 152
    - (b) 135
    - (c) 146
    - (d) 195

12. 1 hundred + 2 tens + 3 ones is equal to ________
    - (a) 124
    - (b) 128
    - (c) 123
    - (d) 122

13. In a book shop there are 381 english novels, 249 comics, 186 story books. Find the total number of books in the shop.
    - (a) 830
    - (b) 816
    - (c) 836
    - (d) 856

14. Which one of the following options is correct ?
    - (a) $7 + 5 > 15 - 2$
    - (b) $18 - 7 < 5 + 4$
    - (c) $20 + 6 = 25 + 15$
    - (d) $18 - 6 > 14 - 3$

15. John scores 5 marks more than the passing marks in his math test. If the passing marks is 33, what marks are scored by John ?
    - (a) 30
    - (b) 28
    - (c) 38
    - (d) 40

Space for Rough Work

16. A man weighed 83 kg, he went for jogging everyday and lost 15 kg weight in 2 months. What is his weight after two months ?

   (a) 63 kg   (b) 56 kg

   (c) 68 kg   (d) 72 kg

17. Find the number obtained after reducing 3 tens from 90.

   (a) 80   (b) 60

   (c) 50   (d) 30

18. Find the fraction of unshaded part in the given figure.

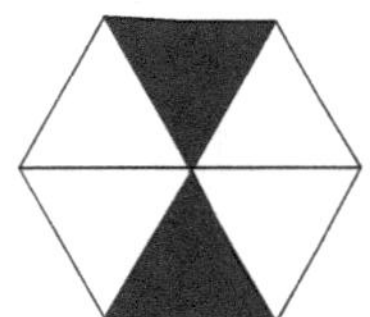

   (a) $\dfrac{2}{6}$ (b) $\dfrac{3}{6}$

   (c) $\dfrac{5}{6}$ (d) $\dfrac{4}{6}$

DIRECTIONS (Qs. 19 & 20) : The ages of all the family members are given in the table. Read the table carefully and answer the following questions.

Father	45 years
Mother	42 years
Grandfather	62 years
Sister	10 years
Brother	18 years
My age	6 years

19. What is the age of father ?

   (a) 60 years   (b) 45 years

   (c) 55 years   (d) 60 years

20. What is the difference between the age of my father and my grandfather ?

   (a) 15 years   (b) 17 years

   (c) 18 years   (d) 20 years

DIRECTIONS (Qs. 21 to 23) : Complete the pattern.

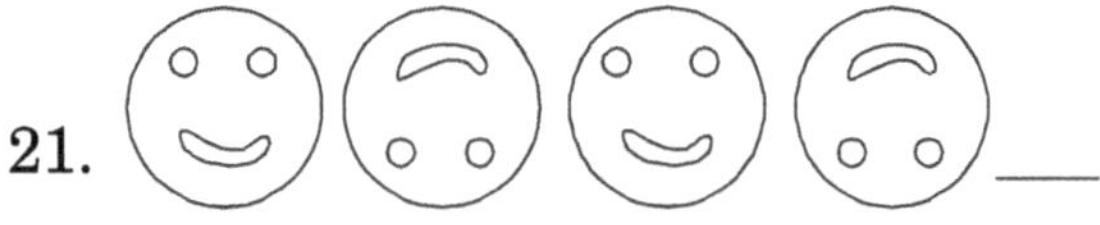

21.

(a)    (b) 

(c)    (d) 

<hr>

Space for Rough Work

22. 12, 17, 22, 27, 32.............

   (a) 37 (b) 40

   (c) 35 (d) 30

23. 27, 25, 23, 21, 19............

   (a) 18 (b) 17

   (c) 20 (d) 21

24. Which number makes the given expression true ?

$$53 - \boxed{} = 16$$

   (a) 38 (b) 37

   (c) 26 (d) 35

25. Which of the following is a cone ?

(a) 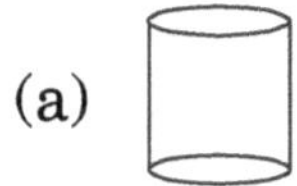 (b) 

(c)  (d) 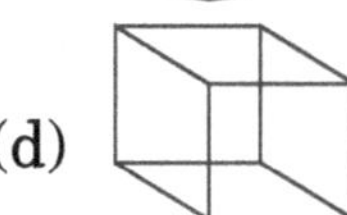

26. In a race competition, Pia runs 20 metres, Naina runs 30 metres and Misha runs 35 metres. How many metres did girls run in all ?

   (a) 80 metres (b) 90 metres

   (c) 85 metres (d) 82 metres

27. Find the fraction of shaded portion.

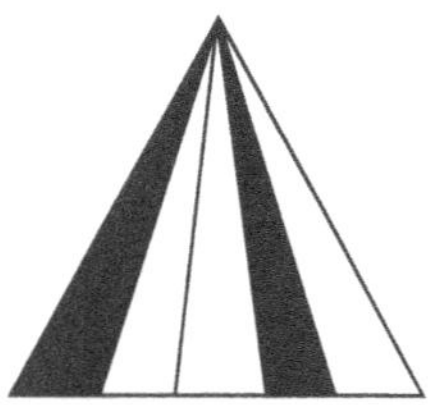

   (a) $\dfrac{2}{5}$ (b) $\dfrac{3}{5}$

   (c) $\dfrac{4}{5}$ (d) 1

28. Ravi bought a bat for ₹535 and a ball for ₹127. How much did he spend in total ?

   (a) ₹662 (b) ₹665

   (c) ₹552 (d) ₹602

29. Which of the following shape is $\dfrac{1}{2}$ part shaded ?

(a) 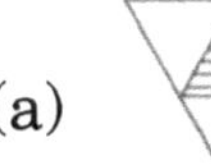 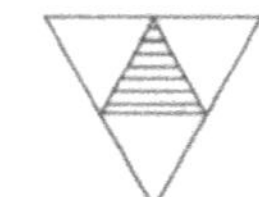 (b) 

(c) 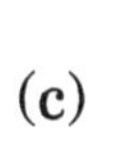 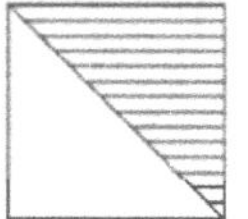 (d) 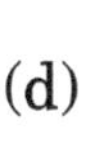 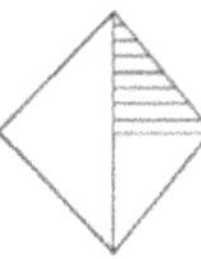

—————————— Space for Rough Work ——————————

30. Rajesh and Suresh are planning to watch a movie on Saturday. Today is Monday, after how many days will they go to watch the movie ?

   (a) 5   (b) 4

   (c) 6   (d) 8

31. What is the missing sign ?

   21 ☐ 7 = 17 − 3

   (a) +   (b) −

   (c) ×   (d) ÷

DIRECTIONS (Qs. 32 to 34) : On the basis of the given diagrams, answer the following questions.

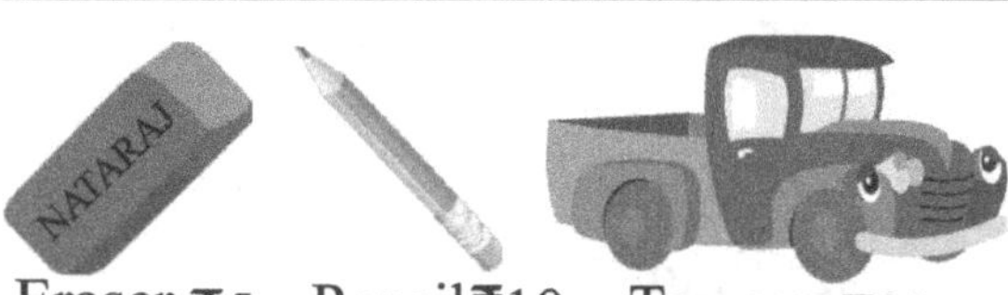

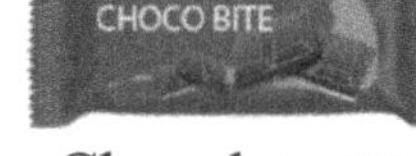

Eraser ₹5   Pencil ₹10   Toy car ₹80

Shirt ₹70   Chocolate ₹70

32. Which of the following costs the least ?

   (a) Eraser   (b) Pencil

   (c) Shirt   (d) Toy car

33. Which of the following costs the most ?

   (a) Pencil   (b) Eraser

   (c) Toy car   (d) Chocolate

34. Which of the following costs ₹10 ?

   (a) Pencil

   (b) Eraser

   (c) Chocolate

   (d) Both (a) & (c)

35. Consider the following statements.

   I: 0 divided by a number gives 0.

   II: Any number divided by itself gives 1.

   Which of the following is correct?

   (a) I is true, but II is false

   (b) I is false, but II is true

   (c) Both are true

   (d) Both are false

OLYMPIAD
Mock Test 5

Name : _____________

Max. Marks : 40

Number of Questions : 40

Time : 2 Hours

There is no negative marking in the test.

1. Find the odd one out from the following.

   99, 90, 10, 20, 50, 60

   (a) 10
   (b) 20
   (c) 99
   (d) 60

2. A fruit basket contains 6 bananas, 2 apples, 1 pineapple and 8 mangoes in a fruit basket. The total numbers of fruits in a basket are ______

   (a) 16
   (b) 15
   (c) 17
   (d) 18

3. Find the place value of 4 in 947.

   (a) 40
   (b) 7
   (c) 90
   (d) 400

4. Find the missing digit.

   445 + ________ = 786

   (a) 351
   (b) 341
   (c) 361
   (d) 391

5. Fill in the missing number.

   657 – _______ = 419

   (a) 220
   (b) 238
   (c) 286
   (d) 262

6. A book shop sold 50 books on Wednesday. On Thursday 10 more books were sold than Wednesday. How many books are sold altogether ?

——————— Space for Rough Work ———————

   (a) 100   (b) 90

   (c) 110   (d) 120

7. If Bulbul studies 8 hours in a day, then how many minutes does she spend per day on her studies?

   (a) 460 minutes

   (b) 470 minutes

   (c) 480 minutes

   (d) 490 minutes

8. 96 beads are used to make a chain. How many beads are needed to make 3 chains?

   (a) 192   (b) 960

   (c) 254   (d) 288

9. What fraction of the given figure is shaded?

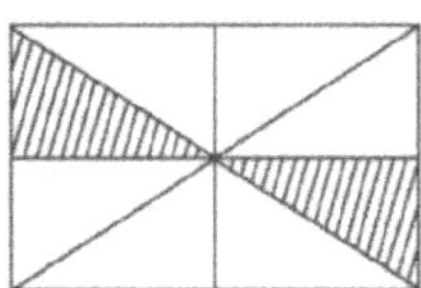

   (a) $\dfrac{2}{4}$ (b) $\dfrac{2}{8}$

   (c) $\dfrac{6}{8}$ (d) $\dfrac{1}{8}$

10. Arpita buys 6 chocolates which costs ₹10 each. How much does 6 chocolates cost?

   (a) ₹50   (b) ₹60

   (c) ₹70   (d) ₹80

11. The total amount of money shown above is ________.

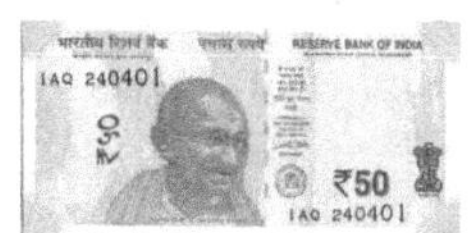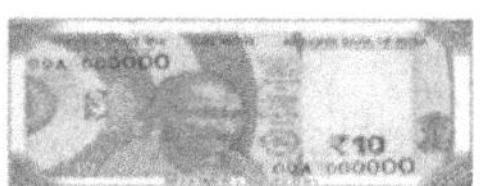

   (a) ₹135   (b) ₹ 38

   (c) ₹125   (d) ₹128

12. The nearest hundred for 534 is __________.

   (a) 500   (b) 600

   (c) 400   (d) 300

13. The calendar shows the month of November.

Sun	Mon	Tue	Wed	Thu	Fri	Sat
	1	2	3	4	5	6
7	8	9	10	11	12	13
14	15	16	17	18	19	20
21	22	23	24	25	26	27
28	29	30				

Space for Rough Work

How many Mondays are there in the month of November ?

(a) 4   (b) 5

(c) 3   (d) 6

14. Anil reached railway station and wait there for 1 hour, the train arrived at 5 : 00 pm. At what time did Anil reached railway station ?

(a) 4 : 00 pm   (b) 4 : 15 am

(c) 5 : 00 am   (d) 5 : 15 pm

15. Radhika wants to buy a videogame which cost ₹205. She has only ₹185. How much more money does she need to buy the video game ?

(a) ₹18   (b) ₹8

(c) ₹20   (d) ₹10

16. Natasha bought a dress for ₹ 568 and a bag for ₹225. How much money the shopkeeper returned, if she gave him ₹800?

(a) ₹10   (b) ₹19

(c) ₹7   (d) ₹9

17. There are 9 books in a bookshelf. Each book has 20 pages. How many pages are there in all ?

(a) 100   (b) 160

(c) 180   (d) 150

18. Identify fraction of the shaded part of the image given below.

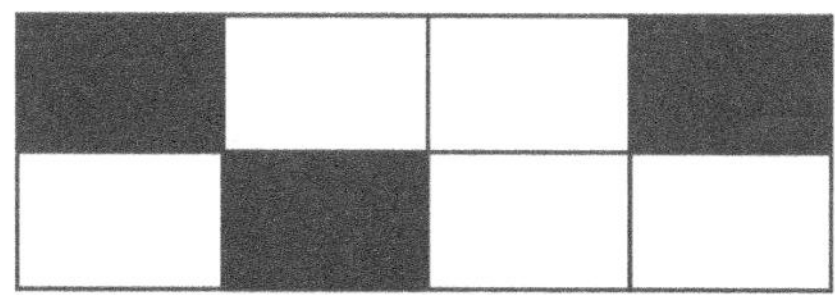

(a) $\dfrac{3}{8}$ (b) $\dfrac{5}{8}$

(c) $\dfrac{4}{8}$ (d) $\dfrac{1}{2}$

19. Sruthi saves ₹2 everyday from her pocket money ? How much does she save in 10 days ?

(a) ₹20   (b) ₹150

(c) ₹18   (d) ₹25

20. The time shown in the clock is

(a) 7 : 15   (b) 7 : 10

(c) 7 : 01   (d) 7 : 02

———————— Space for Rough Work ————————

21. Navya was born on 29th February. Her birthday comes _______.

   (a) every year

   (b) twice in a year

   (c) after every two year

   (d) after every four year

22. Manya and Tanvi are good friends. They went for dance class at 7:00 pm and came back home at 8:00 pm. How much time did they practice dance ?

   (a) 2 hours   (b) 4 hour

   (c) 1 hour   (d) 3 hours

23. The 10 apples weight the same as 2 melon. How many melons would weight the same as 30 apples ?

   (a) 11   (b) 21

   (c) 6   (d) 4

24. Which of the following is a sphere ?

   (a) Ball   (b) Ice cream

   (c) Book   (d) Coca-cola

25. Which of the following is different from other three?

   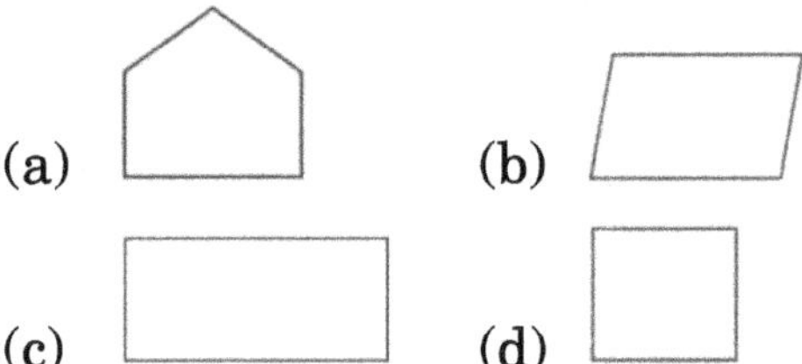

   (a)   (b)   (c)   (d)

26. Complete the pattern.

   ③ ⑥ ⑨ ⑫ ⑮ _____ ㉑

   (a) 16   (b) 17

   (c) 18   (d) 20

27. Which of the following options is correct ?

   (a) 92 = 9 tens and 2 tens

   (b) 67 = 6 tens and 7 tens

   (c) 108 = 100 tens and 8 ones

   (d) 58 = 5 tens and 8 ones

Space for Rough Work

28. How many squares are there in the figure?

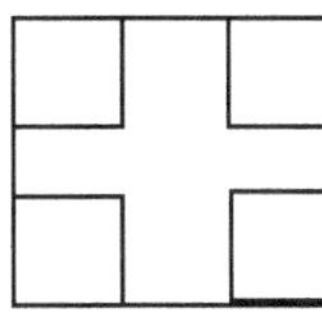

(a) 5   (b) 4

(c) 3   (d) 2

29. A car can travel 60 km in one hour. How much can it travel in 6 hours ?

(a) 360 km   (b) 480 km

(c) 380 km   (d) 350 km

30. Consider the following statements.

Statement - I: Capacity of a bucket is measured in litres.

Statement - II: Weight of a pencil is measured in kilograms.

Now, choose the correct option.

(a) Statements I is true and II is false.

(b) Statements I is false and II is true.

(c) Both statements I and II are true.

(d) Both statements I and II are false.

31. Binu had 24 movie tickets. She distributed them equally among 8 friends. How many movie tickets did each friend get ?

(a) 4   (b) 2

(c) 3   (d) 4

32. Match the columns.

Column - I	Column - II
(A) 14×32	(1) 5×3
(B) $3 + 3 + 3 + 3 + 3$	(2) 0
(C) $0 \times \times 52$	(3) 52
(D) $52 \times \times 1$	(4) $32 \times \times 14$

	A	B	C	D
(a)	4	2	1	3
(b)	3	2	1	4
(c)	3	1	2	4
(d)	4	1	2	3

DIRECTIONS (Qs. 33 to 36) : The table given below shows how do the children in Mala's class come to school?

Means of transport	Cycle	School bus	Car	Walking
Number of children	15	17	2	8

Space for Rough Work

33. How many children do come to school by cycle ?

   (a) 10   (b) 5

   (c) 8   (d) 15

34. Least number of children come by ________ .

   (a) car   (b) bicycle

   (c) school bus   (d) walking

35. Most of the children come by ________ .

   (a) car   (b) bicycle

   (c) school bus   (d) walking

36. How many more children do come by bus than by car ?

   (a) 12   (b) 15

   (c) 17   (d) 10

37. Which of the following balance is correct?

   (a)

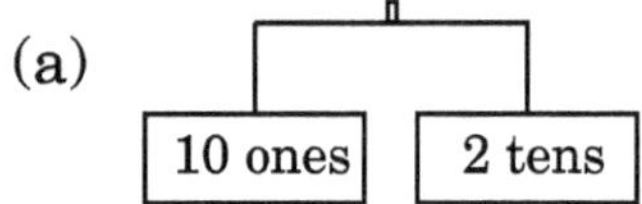

   (b)

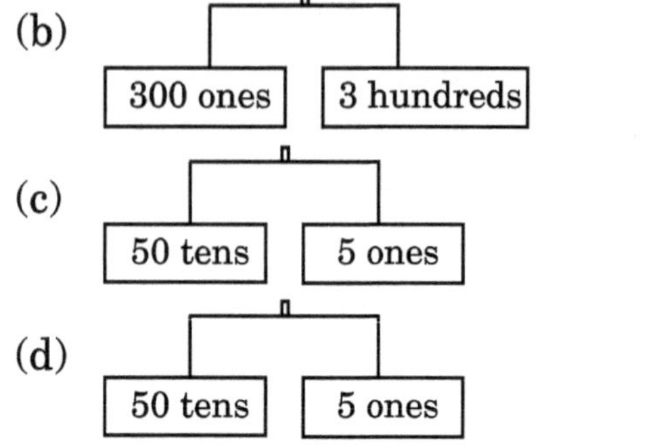

   (c)

   (d)

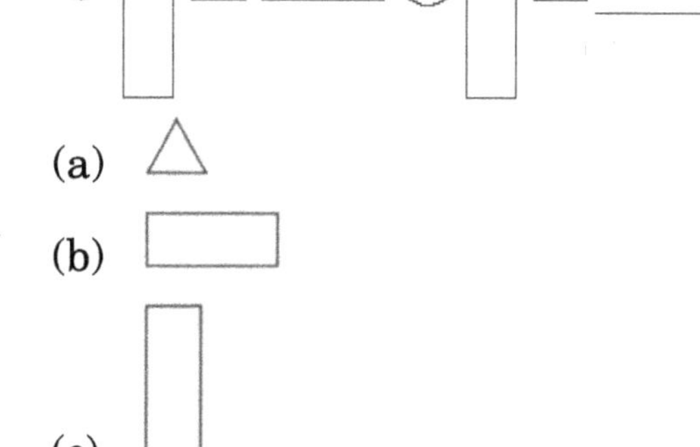

38.

   (a)

   (b)

   (c)

   (d) None of these

39. If Reena's birthday is on 26th July and today is 8th July. How many days are left for her birthday ?

   (a) 16   (b) 8

   (c) 18   (d) 20

40. Which of the following is longest?

   (a) Pencil   (b) Handspan

   (c) Bat   (d) Ruler

SCIENCE MOCK TEST 1-5

OLYMPIAD
Mock Test $\boxed{1}$

Name : __________

Number of Questions : 35

Max. Marks : 35

Time : 2 Hours

There is no negative marking in the test.

1. Which one of the following is the food for the animal given in the picture below?

   (a) Flesh   (b) Fruits

   (c) Vegetables   (d) Rice

2. Identify the picture that can move from one place to another on its own. [2016]

   (a) 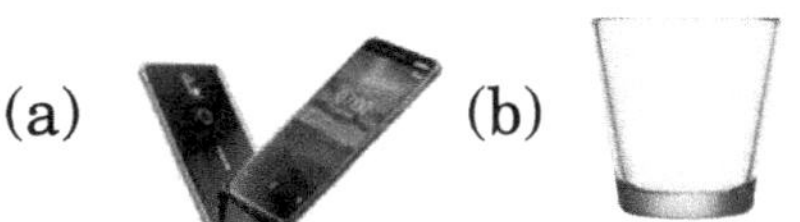   (b)

   (c)    (d)

3. Sarika keeps the tap open while brushing her teeth. This action of Sarika is known as ________ .

   (a) saving of water

   (b) careful use of water

   (c) careless use of water

   (d) none of these

4. Identify the wild animal from the options given below.

   (a)    (b) 

   (goat)   (cow)

Space for Rough Work

(c)  (d) None of these

(hippopotamus)

5. Which one of the following gases of atmosphere is inhaled by human beings to be alive?

(a) Nitrogen

(b) Oxygen

(c) Helium

(d) None of these

6. Which one of the following statements is correct?

Statement 1: Both living and non-living things are important for us.

Statement 2: Only living things are important for us.

(a) Statement 1 is correct.

(b) Statement 2 is correct.

(c) Both statements 1 and 2 are correct.

(d) Both statements 1 and 2 are incorrect.

7. Which of these is a creeper?

(a)    (b) 

Pumpkin   Money plant

(c) 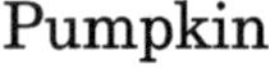   (d) 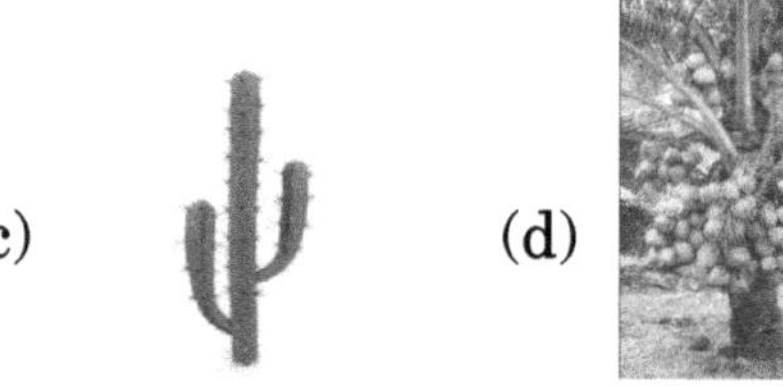

Cactus   Coconut tree

8. Marry found an animal X in a garden. She made the following observations about the animal:

- It has a backbone.
- It has a gills to help it breath.
- It is a plant-eater.

Based on the information above, what is the most likely body covering this animal has ?

(a) Fur   (b) Feathers

(c) Scales   (d) Shell

9. The given figure shows a black box containing an object. Kunal put his hand into the box and made the following comments.

1.   It is cold.

2.   It is rough.

3.   It is hard.

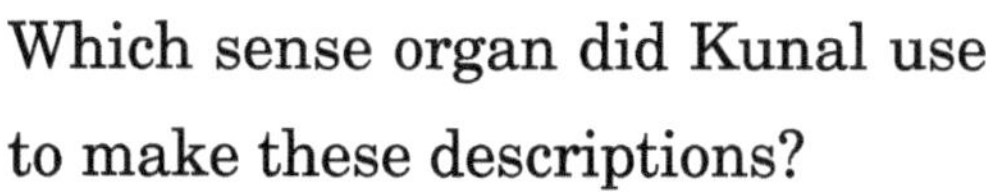

Which sense organ did Kunal use to make these descriptions?

(a) Ear   (b) Skin

(c) Tongue   (d) Nose

10. My father's nephew or niece is my ________ .

(a) cousin

(b) uncle

(c) aunt

(d) brother-in-law

11. The person in the given figure is a/an ________ .

(a) doctor

(b) cobbler

(c) astronaut

(d) carpenter

12. Which part of plant produces food?

(a) Root

(b) Shoot

(c) Stem

(d) Leaves

13. To which place of worship does Sikhs go to pray?

(a) Temple

(b) Mosque

(c) Church

(d) Gurudwara

———— Space for Rough Work ————

14. Which of the following yields fibre?

(a) Barley

(b) Tea

(c) Cotton

(d) Mustard

15. Which of the following is NOT the property of air?

(a) Air fills space.

(b) Air gives shape to things.

(c) Air has weight.

(d) All of these

16. I am two in number, helps to hear the loud noise of aeroplane as well as the soft sound of bird. Guess who am I?

(a) Eye

(b) Ear

(c) Skin

(d) Nose

17. Consider the following statement and choose the correct answer.

Statement 1. We can see the blue sky with our ears.

Statement 2. We can see a butterfly with our eyes.

Statement 3. We can taste a lemon with our tongue.

(a) Statement 1 is true, Statement 2 and 3 are false.

(b) Statement 1 and 2 are true, Statement 3 is false.

(c) Statement 1 is false and Statement 2, 3 are true.

(d) All the statements are true.

18. Kuldeep is a ______. He sells medicines.

(a) tailor

(b) carpenter

(c) doctor

(d) chemist

19. The sunflower turns towards the sun in the morning. This shows that a sunflower can:

(a) grow

(b) reproduce

(c) move

(d) take in air and water

20. Which of the following is a wild animal that eats plants as well as flesh of animals?

(a) Cow   (b) Rabbit

(c) Bear   (d) Goat

21. Study the given flow chart and select the correct option.

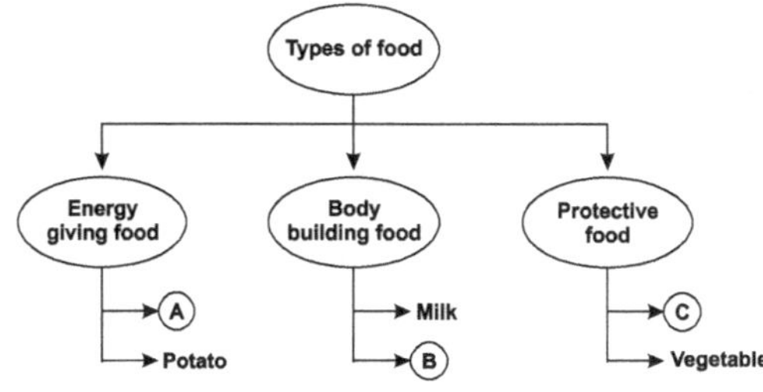

(a) A – Apple B – Bread C – Cheese

(b) A – Rice B – Banana C – Pizza

(c) A – Rice B – Egg C – Apple

(d) A – Grapes B – Apple C – Banana

22. The room of the house shown in the given picture is a _______ .

(a) living room

(b) dining room

(c) kitchen

(d) bedroom

23. Which of following is necessary for human survival?

(a) Air, water and bones

(b) Bones, muscles, and blood

(c) Food, blood and heart

(d) All of these

24. Find the missing alphabet to find out the correct occupation of the man shown in the figure.

(1) A (2) L (3) R

(a) T, I, O

(b) T, A, R

(c) P, E, O

(d) C, B, L

Space for Rough Work

25. Which of the following activities should be avoided in school?

    (a) Run around the benches and don't climb on them.

    (b) Push or pull your friends while playing.

    (c) Follow the rules while playing.

    (d) Both (a) and (b).

26. Which of the following things we should keep in a first aid box?

    (a) Band-aid

    (b) Cotton

    (c) Nail paint

    (d) Both (a) and (b)

27. Which of these is used for mass communication?

    (a) Newspaper

    (b) Radio

    (c) Television

    (d) All of these

28. Which of the following festival is celebrated on 26 January every year?

    (a) Independence Day

    (b) Republic Day

    (c) Gandhi Jayanti

    (d) Teachers Day

29. Identify the personality.

    (a) Mahatma Gandhi

    (b) Kiran Bedi

    (c) Mother Teresa

    (d) Kalpana Chawla

30. What kind of problems can we face, if we never eat green vegetables like spinach, cabbage and beans ?

    (a) Will not get enough fibre in the diet.

    (b) Will be tired always.

    (c) Will be less energetic.

    (d) Will feel sleepy.

———— Space for Rough Work ————

31. Which of the following is an omnivorous animal?

- (a) Cow
- (b) Crow
- (c) Lion
- (d) All of these

32. Which of the following fibres is obtained from plants?

- (a) Cotton
- (b) Jute
- (c) Silk
- (d) Both (a) and (b)

33. Which one of the following organs senses hotness and coldness?

- (a) Eye
- (b) Ear
- (c) Skin
- (d) Nose

34. Shreya lives in 'City of Joy' where rice and fish is the main dish. In which city, she is living?

- (a) Kolkata
- (b) Delhi
- (c) Jaipur
- (d) Mumbai

35. Look at the following monument carefully. In which location it is located?

- (a) Mumbai
- (b) Cochin
- (c) Kolkata
- (d) New Delhi

OLYMPIAD
Mock Test 2

Name : ___________

Number of Questions : 35

Max. Marks : 35

Time : 2 Hours

There is no negative marking in the test.

1. Which of the following organs in human body supplies blood to the whole body?

   (a) 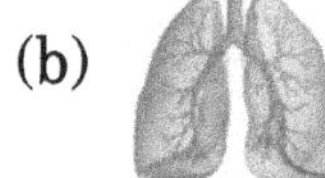
   Heart

   (b) Lungs

   (c) Brain

   (d) All of these

2. David saw an animal that crawls. It feeds on plants only and has an Outer covering of shells.
   Which one of the following animals correctly fits into the description?

   (a) Snail

   (b) Crab

   (c) Snake

   (d) Earthworm

3. Which of the following plants gives us oil?

   (a) Coconut

   (b) Sunflower

   (c) Mustard

   (d) All of these

4. In the absence of which of the materials, plants can not prepare their food?

   (a) Air

   (b) Water

   (c) Animal

   (d) All of these

———— Space for Rough Work ————

5. Which of the following is a natural, non-living thing?

(a) Bird   (b) Car

(c) Chair   (d) River

6. Which of the following we use while crossing the road?

(a) Footpath

(b) Zebra Crossing

(c) Traffic Light

(d) Both (b) and (c)

7. Which of the following organs helps in digestion organ?

(a) Heart   (b) Stomach

(c) Lungs   (d) Kidney

8. Which of the following is a temporary house?

(a) Apartment   (b) Tent

(c) Bungalow   (d) All of these

9. Look at the picture and tell the personality shown in the picture is famous in which of the following fields?

(a) Cricket

(b) Science

(c) Music

(d) All of these

10. We can get a living organism from which of the following non-living things?

(a) Egg   (b) Pencil

(c) Kite   (d) Apple

<hr>

Space for Rough Work

11. Which of the following articles should not be touched with wet hands?

(a) Toys

(b) Knite

(c) Gas stove

(d) Electric switch

12. Look at the picture and tell which season does this picture depict?

(a) Summer   (b) Winter

(c) Rainy   (d) Snowfall

13. Mark 'T' for true sentence and 'F' for false sentence.

(1) Eat fresh food.

(2) Always keep prepared food open.

(3) Food keep us strong and healthy.

(a) TTT   (b) TFT

(c) FTF   (d) FFT

14. Which of the following do you need, if you want your school uniform to be stiched?

(a) Fabric

(b) Tailor

(c) Bucket

(d) Both (a) and (b)

15. Which of the following house can cause disease?

(a) A house with many mem-bers.

(b) A house without windows and doors.

(c) A clean house.

(d) A house with sufficient water and air supply.

16. Imran is very happy because today is Eid and he will get meethi sewaiyan to eat. All his relatives will meet and go to pray their God. In which of the following places they will go for worship?

(a) Mosque (b) Restaurant

(c) Church (d) Temple

17. We can send parcels and letters to different places through ________.

(a) airways

(b) post office

(c) railways

(d) waterways

18. If some guests are about to arrive and your house is very dirty, whom you will call to help your mother?

(a) Watchman

(b) Milkman

(c) Housekeeper

(d) Teacher

19. The __________stores urine before expelling it out.

(a) kidney (b) bladder

(c) stomach (d) liver

20. Which of the following games needs maximum four players to be played?

(a) Cricket (b) Carrom

(c) Chess (d) Tennis

21. Which of the following is not a fruit?

(a) Rose (b) Tomato

(c) Pineapple (d) Both (a) and (b)

22. Look at the picture and tell what can you say about the animals shown in the figure.

Horse Cow Bufallo

(a) They are wild animals.

(b) They are domestic animals.

(c) They are useful for human beings.

(d) Both (b) and (c)

23. Which of the following is an incorrect match?

(a) Lion : Omnivorous

(b) Cow : Domestic

(c)   Goat : Herbivore

(d)   Bees : Hive

24. Group 1: Bullock cart, boat and bicycle.

Group 2: Airplane and train.

Consider the groups of vehicles and choose the correct answer.

(a)   **Group 1:** Slowest means of transport.

    Group 2: Vehicles run on land.

(b)   **Group 1:** Fastest means of transport.

    Group 2: Used for long distances.

(c)   **Group 1:** Slowest means of transport.

    Group 2: Vehicles used for long distances.

(d)   **Group 1:** Public means of transport.

    Group 2: Used only in cities.

25. What do you call a scientist that studies life?

(a)   Physicist

(b)   Biologist

(c)   Geologist

(d)   Meteorologist

26. Match the following.

A.	Gateway of India	p.	Delhi
B.	Howrah Bridge	q.	Mumbai
C.	Marina beach	r.	Kolkata
D.	Lal Quila	s.	Chennai

	A	B	C	D
(a)	q	r	s	p
(b)	p	q	r	s
(c)	r	s	q	p
(d)	s	p	q	r

27. Which organ of body is shown in the figure?

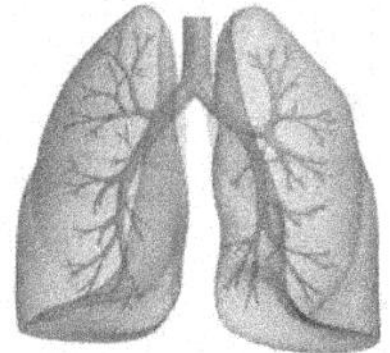

(a)   Heart   (b)   Lungs

(c)   Kidneys   (d)   Stomach

28. Which of the following is water-proof as well as transparent?

(a) Rubber

(b) Glass

(c) Wood

(d) All of these

29. Which of the following we get from plants?

(a) Cotton

(b) Fruits

(c) Jute

(d) All of these

30. Which of the following you should do to keep your clothes germs free?

(a) Wash them with good detergent.

(b) Do not wear them.

(c) Let them dry in the sun.

(d) Both (a) and (c)

31. The picture given below shows children wearing suitable to wear in winter season.

Which of these gives fibres used to make a sweater?

(a)    (b) 

(c)    (d) 

32. Which of the following is used to produce silk?

(a) Catterpiler

(b) Butterfly

(c) Silkworm

(d) All of these

33. We eat leaves of some plants. Which are they?

(a) Coriander

(b) Spinach

(c) Cabbage

(d) Both (a) and (b)

34. Choose odd one out.

    (a) Milk   (b) Oil

    (c) Cheese   (d) Water

35. Which of the following is not true about city Mumbai?

    (a) Gateway of India is located here.

    (b) People celebrate Ganesh Chaturthi here.

    (c) It is one of the metro cities.

    (d) People of Mumbai speaks Tamil.

OLYMPIAD
Mock Test 3

Name : __________
Number of Questions : 35

Max. Marks : 35
Time : 2 Hours

There is no negative marking in the test.

1. Sravan said, "It's hot". He is using his sense of _______ to gather information.

    (a) sight
    (b) smell
    (c) touch
    (d) hearing

2. Our muscles interact with _______ to allow movement.

    (a) arms
    (b) feet
    (c) knee
    (d) bones

3. Salt is added to ice to

    (a) melt it.
    (b) make it evaporate.
    (c) make it harder.
    (d) turn to gas.

4. Which of the following is not obtained from plants?

    (a) Wooden chair
    (b) Book
    (c) Bicycle
    (d) Rubber

5. Which of the following statements is true about the house given below?

    (a) It is a temporary house.
    (b) It is made up of canvas.
    (c) It can be easily moved from one place to another place.
    (d) All of the above

Space for Rough Work

6. Which of the following is NOT a living thing?

(a) 

Clouds

(b) 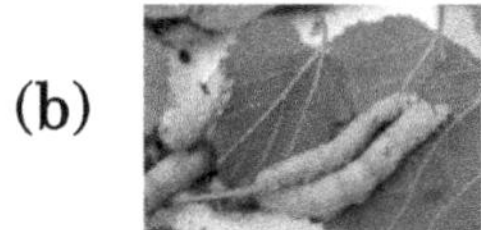

Silkworm larva

(c) 

Grass

(d) 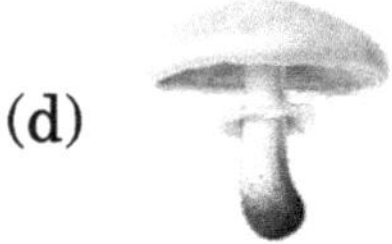

Mushroom

7. What does an anemometer measure?

(a) Wind speed

(b) Temperature

(c) Air Pressure

(d) Rainfall

8. Which of the following forms of water is steam?

(a) Solid

(b) Liquid

(c) Gas

(d) None of these

9. Which of the following fruits is seedless?

(a) Orange   (b) Banana

(c) Mango   (d) Papaya

10. The man in the figure given below is a

(a) traffic policeman

(b) doctor

(c) policeman

(d) watch man

11. Which kind of clothes should be worn while lighting crackers?

   (a) Nylon   (b) Polyester

   (c) Rayon   (d) Cotton

12. Which of the following things can grow?

(a)    (b) 

(c)    (d) 

13. Which of the following is an incorrect match?

   (a) Wheat : Egg

   (b) Milk : Paneer

   (c) Tree : Wood

   (d) Peanuts : Oil

14. Which of the following diagrams shows the correct sequence?

(a) 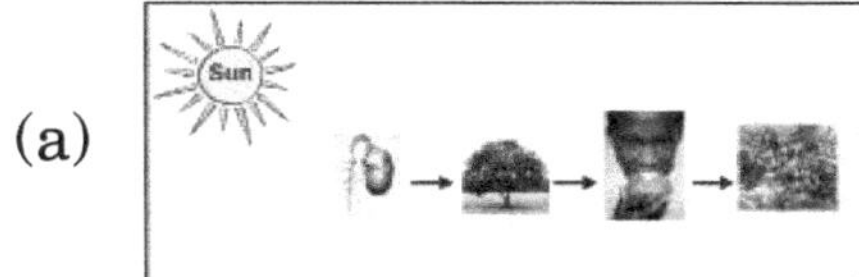

(b) 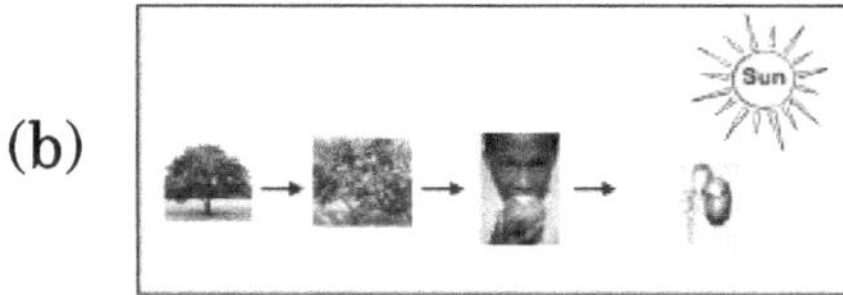

(c) 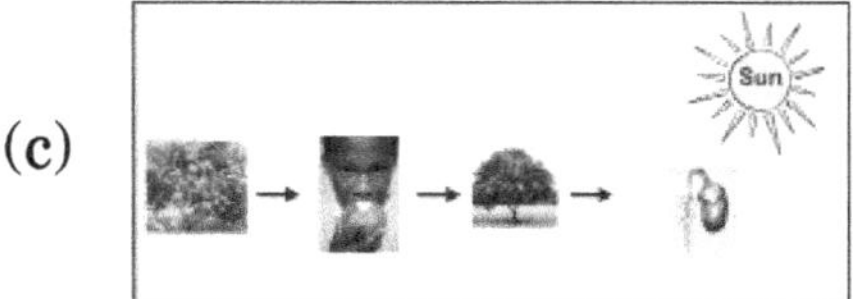

(d) 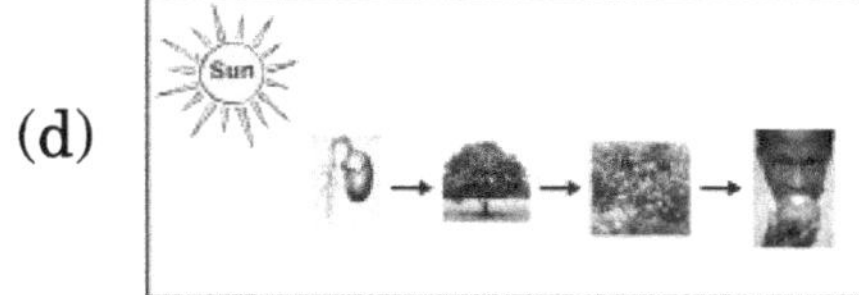

15. Birds are the only animals that have ________.

   (a) wings   (b) legs

   (c) tails   (d) all of these

Space for Rough Work

16. Which of the following defines evaporation?

(a) Changing ice into water by heating.

(b) Changing ice into water vapour by heating.

(c) Changing water into ice by cooling.

(d) Changing water into water vapour by heating.

17. Which of these are protective foods?

(a) Grapes

(b) Broccoli

(c) Oranges

(d) All of these

18. Throwing factory waste material and garbage into the rivers, ponds and seas will cause ________.

(a) water pollution

(b) malaria

(c) death of marine animals

(d) Both (a) and (c)

19. Meat of pig is called ________.

(a) pork

(b) mutton

(c) beef

(d) chicken

20. Match the following animals with their uses.

Animals	Uses
(A) Horse	1. House keeping
(B) Dogs	2. Wool
(C) Sheep	3. Mutton
(D) Goat	4. Travelling

	A	B	C	D
(a)	1	3	2	4
(b)	2	1	3	4
(c)	4	1	2	3
(d)	3	2	1	4

21. Which of the following is not dangerous?

(a)  Touching an electric gadget.

(b) 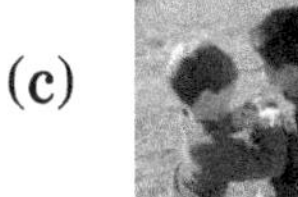 Playing with broken toys.

(c)  Pushing each other

(d) Walking on the footpath

22. Which of the following is known for changing colours?

(a) Frog

(b) Superworm

(c) Alligator

(d) Chameleon

23. What do you call the series of changes that many animals go through in life?

(a) The circle of life

(b) Food Chain

(c) A life cycle

(d) Period of life

24. I have so many windows and doors. People can sleep, eat, play and walk on me while travelling from one place to another. I run on tracks. Identify who I am?

(a) Airplane

(b) Train

(c) Bus

(d) None of these

25. Sending and receiving of spoken or written messages between people is called ________.

(a) communication

(b) transportation

(c) transformation

(d) conversation

26. It is usually cool in the morning, gets warmer at noon and it gets cool and pleasant in the evening. What phenomena I am talking about?

(a) Flood

(b) Earthquake

(c) Weather

(d) Season

27. Look at the picture and choose the correct option.

What can you say about the animal shown in the picture?

(a) It is not a wild animal.

(b) This have poor sense of hearing.

(c) This have poor sense of smell.

(d) The animal has no bones.

28. Choose odd one out.

(a) Kidney

(b) Lungs

(c) Stomach

(d) Ears

29. Choose odd one out.

(a) Air   (b) Book

(c) Glass jar   (d) Bubble

30. What is the common feature of a bear (animal), a crow (bird) and a jackal (animal)?

(a) They are herbivores.

(b) They are carnivores.

(c) They are omnivores.

(d) They are vultures.

31. What do you mean by 'Beast of Burden'?

(a) Walking animals

(b) Running animals

(c) Working animals

(d) Laughing animals

32. Which of the following non-living things is very crucial for the survival of living beings?
  (a) Rubber
  (b) Air
  (c) Water
  (d) Both (b) and (c)

33. Plants which grow on the land is called ________.
  (a) Omnivorous plant
  (b) Aquatic plant
  (c) Terrestrial plant
  (d) Aerial plant

34. Which of the following activities you can perform without water?
  (a) Cook
  (b) Dance
  (c) Swim
  (d) Clean house

35. Which of the following groups of things is not the plant product?
  (a) Cotton, jute, silk
  (b) Orange, cereals, paper
  (c) Nylon, honey, plastic
  (d) Pulses, rice, nuts

Name : __________   Max. Marks : 40

Number of Questions : 40   Time : 2 Hours

There is no negative marking in the test.

1. When a baby is borne, it has about ________.

   (a) 230 bones

   (b) 300 bones

   (c) 150 bones

   (d) 450 bones

2. Match the column:

Column (i)	Column (ii)
A. Eye	p. Taste
B. Ear	q. See
C. Nose	r. Hear
D. Tongue	s. Smell

	A	B	C	D
(a)	q	r	s	p
(b)	q	s	p	r
(c)	p	q	r	s
(d)	s	r	q	p

3. Which of the following fabrics protects us from cold?

   (a) Cotton   (b) Silk

   (c) Wool   (d) Nylon

4. Which of the following shows the direction of the wind?

   (a) Windmill

   (b) Wall clock

   (c) Rain gauge

   (d) Magnetic needle

—————— *Space for Rough Work* ——————

5. Choose the odd one out.

    (a) Radio   (b) Newspaper

    (c) Television   (d) Aeroplane

6. Names of some foods are given below. How many energy-giving food are there?

apple, butter, milk, pulses, rice, sugar

    (a) 5   (b) 3

    (c) 4   (d) 6

7. Wet clothes dry under sun. This is an example of _______ .

    (a) condensation

    (b) melting

    (c) boiling

    (d) evaporation

8. Find the missing alphabets to find out the correct occupation of the man shown in the figure.

    (1) O (2) T M (3) N

    (a) P, M, S

    (b) P, S, A

    (c) P, M, A

    (d) P, S, M

9. Match the celebration with the dates:

Celebrations	Date
A. Republic Day	p. 26 January
B. Teacher's Day	q. 2 October
C. Gandhi Jayanti	r. 14 November
D. Children's Day	s. 5 September

	A	B	C	D
(a)	q	r	p	s
(b)	p	q	r	s
(c)	p	s	q	r
(d)	q	p	r	s

10. Which of the following transports have more than 4 wheels?

    (a) Bus   (b) Cycle

    (c) Train   (d) Car

Space for Rough Work

11. Which of the following is a pair of water transport?

   (a) Boat and train

   (b) Boat and car

   (c) Boat and ship

   (d) Boat and bus

DIRECTIONS (Qs. 12 to 16): Select the odd one out.

12. (a) Tulsi   (b) Neem
     (c) Mint   (d) Coriander

13. (a) Cat   (b) Dog
     (c) Rabbit   (d) Giraffe

14. (a) Cotton   (b) Jute
     (c) Silk   (d) Socks

15. (a) Television   (b) Radio
     (c) Newspaper   (d) Telephone

16. (a) Raincoat   (b) Monsoon
     (c) Winter   (d) Summer

17. The monument shown is situated in

(Victoria Memorial)

   (a) New Delhi   (b) Mumbai

   (c) Kolkata   (d) Jaipur

18. Which of the following is a permanent house?

(a) 

Igloo

(b) 

Bungalow

(c) 

Caravan

(d) 

Tent

19. Choose the correct answer from the following statements.

Statement A: The sun changes its shape.

Statement B: The moon does not have its own light.

Statement C: We can count the number of stars.

(a) Statement A is true, Statement B and C are false.

(b) Statement A and C are true, Statement B is false.

(c) Statement A and C are false, Statement B is true.

(d) Statement A and B are true, Statement C is false.

20. What time of day is usually the warmest?

(a) The afternoon

(b) Night time

(c) Dawn

(d) Evening

21. While camping, you decided to build a fire. Which component of the fire is an example of a gas?

(a) The smoke coming from the fire.

(b) The actual fire itself.

(c) The logs on the fire.

(d) The water to put the fire out.

22. A rainbow is visible in which of the following seasons?

(a) Summer   (b) Winter

(c) Spring   (d) Monsoon

23. Which one of the following eats flesh from dead body of the living organism?

(a) Penguins   (b) Parrots

(c) Pigeon   (d) Scavengers

24. A house protects us from ______.

(a) heat   (b) cold

(c) rain   (d) all of these

25. Ravi is a carpenter. He ______.

(a) makes door

(b) repairs furniture

(c) repairs pipes

(d) both (a) and (b)

—————————— *Space for Rough Work* ——————————

26. There is fire in Rohan's house. In such a case where should his father call?

    (a) Police Station

    (b) Hospital

    (c) Fire Station

    (d) Jal board

27. Which of these statements is true?

    (a) Diwali is the festival of light and crackers.

    (b) Guruparava is celebrated by Sikh.

    (c) Jesus Christ's birthday is celebrated as Christmas.

    (d) All of these

28. Which of the following activities keeps bones and muscles strongs?

    (a) Brushing   (b) Bathing

    (c) Exercise   (d) Eating

29. Which of the following is NOT a good habit?

    (a) Cross the road using zebra crossing.

    (b) Stand in a line before getting into a bus.

    (c) Put your hand or head out of the window.

    (d) None of these

30. Which of the following animal lives in jungle?

    (a) Tiger   (b) Buffalo

    (c) Hen   (d) Cat

31. A student carried out an experiment as shown in the figure given below.

Which is the best conclusion drawn from the above experiment?

    (a) Air moves things

    (b) Air is needed for burning

    (c) Air occupies space

    (d) Air has weight

32. Which of the following is an example of root?

    (a) Carrot

    (b) Pineapple

    (c) Radish

    (d) Both (a) and (c)

33. ![spoon] is made up of _______.

(a) wood   (b) rubber

(c) metal   (d) glass

34. A mechanic repairs _______.

(a) wooden furniture

(b) iron pipes

(c) clothes

(d) cehicles

35. Which of the following personalities is related with the field of science?

(a) Rabindranath Tagore

(b) Bill gates

(c) Mahatma Gandhi

(d) Albert Einstein

36. Which of the following do not have a definite shape?

(a) Book

(b) Ice

(c) Smoke

(d) Milk

37. Look at the figure given below. Which of the following is used in such situation?

(a) Woollen clothes

(b) Rain coat

(c) Cotton clothes

(d) Silk clothes

38. Which of the following persons wears uniform?

(a) Sweeper

(b) Policeman

(c) Lawyer

(d) Both (b) & (c)

39. What does the following figure represent?

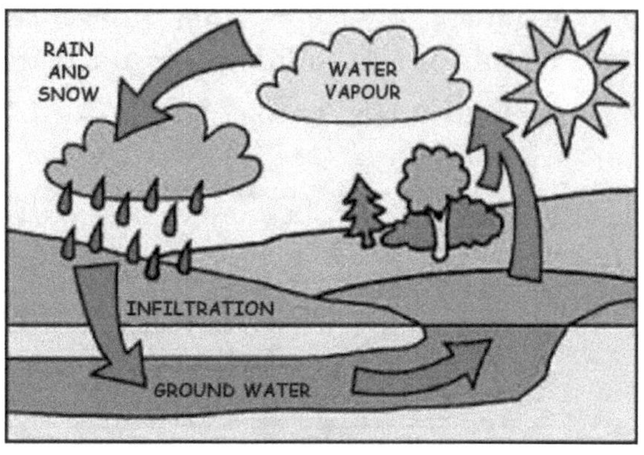

(a) Path of germs in air

(b) Water cycle

(c) Storm

(d) Formation of clouds

40. If a steel plate is kept on top of a hot vessel, we see tiny droplets of water on the plate. Which of these get converted into water droplets?

(a) Ice   (b) Dew

(c) Steam   (d) Smoke

OLYMPIAD
Mock Test 5

Name : __________   Max. Marks : 40

Number of Questions : 40   Time : 2 Hours

There is no negative marking in the test.

1. Which of the following will change with the change in season?

    (a) Types of clothes we wear.

    (b) Variety of fruits and vegetables in the market.

    (c) Types of house in which we live.

    (d) Both (a) and (b)

2. Which of the following flowers moves in the direction of the sun?

    (a) Rose

    (b) Sunflower

    (c) Jasmine

    (d) All of these

3. Which one of the following nutrients helps in growth of the body?

    (a) Vitamins

    (b) Proteins

    (c) Fats

    (d) Carbohydrates

4. Which of the following numbers do we dial to speak to the police, if there is an emergency?

    (a) 141

    (b) 100

    (c) 101

    (d) 120

———————————— *Space for Rough Work* ————————————

5. Which of the following is a festival celebrated by the people in Chennai?

(a) Bihu   (b) Pongal

(c) Durga Puja   (d) Chat puja

6. Helpers like milkman, watchman and housekeeper make our lives ______ and ______. We must respect them.

(a) easy and profitable

(b) profitable and comfortable

(c) easy and playful

(d) easy and comfortable

7. Types of clothes we wear, depend on which of the following factors?

(a) Climate

(b) Family

(c) Oceasion

(d) Both (a) and (c)

8. On which of the following occassions, the Prime Minister, the President and several other people visit Raj Ghat and offer flowers and do prayer?

(a) Gandhi Jayanti

(b) Republic day

(c) Mahavir Jayanti

(d) Independence day

9. Which of the following you will play in the playground?

(a) Cricket

(b) Carrom

(c) Ludo

(d) Both (a) and (b)

10. How does snake eat insects?

(a) Chewing

(b) Swallowing

(c) Crushing

(d) None of these

11. Which of the following is TRUE about lion?

(a) Lion is a wild animal.

(b) Lion is a carnivorous animal.

(c) Lion is an omnivorous animal.

(d) Both (a) and (b)

———————————— Space for Rough Work ————————————

12. At home, we should stay away from which of the following things?

(a)    (b) 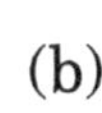

(c)    (d) Both (a) and (b)

13. How many means of mass communication can you see in the given picture.

(a) 4   (b) 5

(c) 6   (d) 3

14. People prefer to wear me in summers. I am a natural fibre.

I absorb sweat and easy to wash. Who I am?

(a) Silk clothes

(b) Cotton clothes

(c) Nylon clothes

(d) Woollen clothes

15. Which of the following is the role of brain?

(a) Help us to think

(b) Removes waste

(c) Pumps blood

(d) Helps us to breathe

16. Observe the figure carefully. What will happen, if a glass is put over a burning candle?

(a) The candle keeps burning.

(b) The candle will stop burning.

(c) The candle shrinks in size.

(d) None of these

17. Ice is called the _______ state of water.

(a) gaseous

(b) solid

(c) liquid

(d) both (a) and (b)

Space for Rough Work

18. Which of the following is not a source of drinking water?

(a) Tap   (b) Sea water

(c) Hand pump   (d) Well

19. Which of the following is an organ of the respiratory system?

(a) Lungs   (b) Stomach

(c) Skull   (d) Heart

20. Fast and strong winds are known as ________.

(a) breeze

(b) storm

(c) wind

(d) earthquake

21. Which of the following is not located in Delhi?

(a) 

Qutub Minar

(b) 

Taj Mahal

(c) 

India Gate

(d)

Red Fort

22. Which of the following is a characteristic of a plant?

(a) It can breathe.

(b) It can grow.

(c) It can reproduce.

(d) All of these

23. Which of the following was the president of India as well as a famous scientist of India?

(a) Dr. A.P.J. Abdul Kalam

(b) Sachin Tendulkar

(c) Mother Teresa

(d) Shahrukh Khan

———— Space for Rough Work ————

24. Fibres like cotton, jute and silk are called _______ because they are not created by man using chemicals.

(a) natural fibres

(b) man-made fibres

(c) useful fibres

(d) handloom fibres

25. Which of the following is the fastest but the most expensive mode of transport?

(a) Landways (b) Airways

(c) Waterways (d) Railways

26. Which of the following is a house on wheels?

(a) Igloo (b) Hut

(c) Tent (d) Caravan

27. Which one of the following reduces with sweating?

(a) Body temperature

(b) Headache

(c) Bleeding

(d) None of these

28. What is the function of skeleton system?

(a) It helps us to think and remember.

(b) It gives shape and support to our body.

(c) It helps us to digest food.

(d) It helps in throwing out the waste from the body.

29. Which of the following shows the direction of the wind?

(a) Windmill

(b) Weather cock

(c) Rainguage

(d) Kite

30. Which of the following make us ill?

(a) Fruits (b) Germs

(c) Vegetables (d) Nuts

31. Which of the following is true or false?

(A) Chew your food well.

(B) We get honey from plants.

(C) Rain is the main source of water.

(D) Do not waste food.

(a) TTTT   (b) TFFT

(c) TFTF   (d) TFTT

32. What can you say about the animal in the picture?

(a) Elephant is a herbivorous animal.

(b) Elephant is a carnivorous animal.

(c) Elephant is an omnivorous animal.

(d) None of these

33. Read the following lines and try to figure out which season I am talking about?

(A) It lasts from November to February.

(B) Some of us use room heaters.

(C) We wear clothes like sweaters, caps, gloves, etc.

(a) Monsoon

(b) Winters

(c) Summers

(d) None of these

34. Look at the figure given below.

Man flying using a parachute

Which of the following makes the man to move?

(a) Water   (b) Air

(c) Electricity   (d) Petrol

Space for Rough Work
---

35. What does the following picture represent?

(a) Internet — Means of mass communication.

(b) Computer — An electronic machine.

(c) A beautiful painting.

(d) Both (a) and (b)

36. What is the main source of heat and light on earth?

(a) Sun   (b) Moon

(c) Star   (d) All of these

37. Raja lives with his father, mother, sister and grandfather. Which kind of family is this?

(a) Small family

(b) Big family

(c) Joint family

(d) None of these

38. Which of the following can be eaten only after cooling?

(a) Cucumber   (b) Rice

(c) Radish   (d) Carrot

39. Which of the following absorbs water from the soil to help the plants to grow?

(a) Roots   (b) Stem

(c) Flower   (d) Leaves

40. Which of the following cannot be reused again and again?

(a) Coal

(b) Petrol

(c) Wood

(d) Both (a) & (b)

GENERAL KNOWLEDGE MOCK TEST 1-5

OLYMPIAD
Mock Test

1

Name : __________

Number of Questions : 25

Max. Marks : 25

Time : 1 Hour

There is no negative marking in the test.

1. Which part of human body is shown in the image given below?

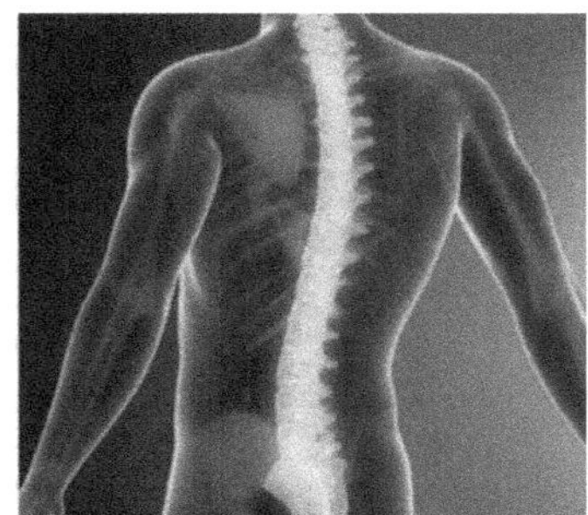

(a) Spinal Cord (b) Skull
(c) Ribs (d) Lungs

2. Which of the following is an aquatic animal?
(a) Giant Panda (b) Zebra
(c) Deer (d) Penguin

3. Which of the following is body building food?
(a) Meat (b) Potato
(c) Pizza (d) Fruits

4. How many lungs does the human body have?
(a) One (b) Two
(c) Three (d) Four

5. The animal shown in the image below is found in ____________ .

(a) Australia

(b) Brazil

(c) New Zealand

(d) South Africa

Space for Rough Work

6. ______________ is the capital of Japan.

   (a) Shanghai   (b) Hiroshima

   (c) Osaka   (d) Tokyo

7. The image shown below is the national flag of ____________.

   (a) France

   (b) Bangladesh

   (c) China

   (d) Japan

8. Which of the following is the largest flower in the world?

   (a) Sunflower

   (b) Marigold

   (c) Tulip

   (d) Rafflesia

9. Which of the following sports does not use a ball?

   (a) Cricket

   (b) Hockey

   (c) Golf

   (d) Ice Hockey

10. With which of the following sports is Geeta Phogat related to?

   (a) Hockey   (b) Wrestling

   (c) Weightlifting (d) Boxing

11. Which of the following planet is known as the Red Planet?

   (a) Mars   (b) Venus

   (c) Moon   (d) Saturn

12. What is the capital of Kerala?

   (a) Kozhikode

   (b) Kochi

   (c) Kovalum

   (d) Thiruvananthapuram

———————— Space for Rough Work ————————

13. Which is the smallest Indian state in terms of area?

(a) Punjab   (b) Sikkim

(c) Goa   (d) Tripura

14. Which of the following bird does not build its own nest?

(a) Parrot   (b) Crow

(c) Cuckoo   (d) Sparrow

15. Which of the following birds has a long pouched beak?

(a) Parrot   (b) Crow

(c) Sparrow   (d) Pelican

16. Which is the highest mountain in the world?

(a) Mount Kailash

(b) Nanda Devi Mountain

(c) Mount Everest

(d) Mount K2

17. A piece of land that is surrounded by water from all sides is known as ________________.

(a) lake   (b) island

(c) pond   (d) coast

18. How many types of lights are there on a traffic signal?

(a) One   (b) Two

(c) Three   (d) Four

19. Before crossing the road, we should always check that ____________.

(a) Traffic Light is red

(b) All vehicles have stopped

(c) There is a zebra crossing

(d) All of the above

20. Young one of a monkey is called ____________________.

(a) Puppy   (b) Kitten

(c) Kid   (d) Infant

21. Which sport uses a net, a racket and a shuttlecock?

(a) Tennis   (b) Badminton

(c) Table Tennis   (d) Squash

Space for Rough Work

22. Where did Jallianwala Bagh massacre take place?

(a) Bangalore   (b) New Delhi

(c) Amritsar   (d) Lucknow

23. Which of the following cities is also known as 'The Pink City'?

(a) Delhi

(b) Agra

(c) Mumbai

(d) Jaipur

24. Which of the following animals is a 'carnivore'?

(a) Tiger

(b) Sheep

(c) Reindeer

(d) Horse

25. Read statements I and II carefully. Choose the correct answer from given options.

Statement I: 'Garba' is a folk dance of Maharashtra.

Statement II: 'Dandiya' is a folk dance of Gujarat.

(a) Only statement I is true.

(b) Only statement II is true.

(c) Both statements are true.

(d) Both statements are false.

Space for Rough Work

OLYMPIAD
Mock Test 2

Name : ___________

Number of Questions : 25

Max. Marks : 25

Time : 1 Hour

There is no negative marking in the test.

1. A dry land area with lots of sand, camel and cactus is called ___________________.

   (a) mountain   (b) island

   (c) desert   (d) plain

2. How many colours are present in the Indian flag (including the Ashok chakra)?

   (a) 3   (b) 2

   (c) 1   (d) 4

3. ___________________ cover more than two third of earth's surface.

   (a) Mountains   (b) Oceans

   (c) Rivers   (d) Islands

4. On a traffic signal, a red light indicates that traffic must _______.

   (a) start

   (b) stop

   (c) wait

   (d) get ready

5. Pavements alongside the roads are meant for _______________.

   (a) walking

   (b) advertising

   (c) sleeping

   (d) driving

6. Traffic rules help us to _______.

   (a) reduce accidents

   (b) save lives

   (c) avoid traffic jams

   (d) all of the above

Space for Rough Work

7. In which of the following seasons we see lots of flowers?

(a) Summer   (b) Winter

(c) Autumn   (d) Spring

8. In which season of the year trees shed their leaves?

(a) Summer   (b) Winter

(c) Autumn   (d) Spring

9. How much time does the earth take to complete one rotation around its axis?

(a) 1 day   (b) 7 days

(c) 30 days   (d) 365 days

10. Which of the following is the national anthem of India?

(a) Jana Gana Mana

(b) Vande Mataram

(c) Jai Jawan Jai Kisan

(d) Saare Jahan Se Achha

11. Humans need _________________ for breathing.

(a) Carbon Dioxide

(b) Oxygen

(c) Ozone

(d) Nitrogen

12. Which of the following is NOT a basic need of living beings?

(a) Sunlight   (b) Recreation

(c) Air   (d) Water

13. Which of the following continents is known as a cold desert?

(a) Asia

(b) Antarctica

(c) Africa

(d) North America

14. Which Indian politician served three terms as the Prime Minister?

(a) A.P.J. Abdul Kalam

(b) Manmohan Singh

(c) Atal Bihari Vajpayee

(d) Jawahar Lal Nehru

15. Which continent has only one country?

(a) Asia   (b) Antarctica

(c) Australia   (d) Europe

16. Which state has been affected by flood recently in August, 2018?

(a) Mumbai

(b) Goa

(c) Delhi

(d) Kerala

———————— Space for Rough Work ————————

17. Who is the current Prime Minister of India?

(a) Rahul Gandhi

(b) Sonia Gandhi

(c) Narendra Modi

(d) Arvind Kejriwal

18. Which of the following insects cause dengue fever?

(a)    (b)

(c)   (d) 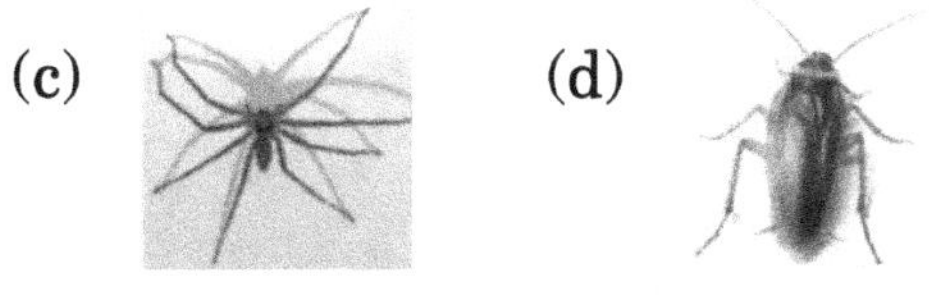

19. Hair in our nose help in stopping _______________ to enter our body.

(a) air

(b) dust particles

(c) carbon dioxide

(d) smoke

20. Rice and wheat are rich in ______ .

(a) carbohydrate

(b) protein

(c) fat

(d) vitamin

21. Butter is rich in ____________ .

(a) Carbohydrate

(b) Fat

(c) Protein

(d) Vitamin

22. What is the function of heart in the human body?

(a) Transport vitamins

(b) Fight diseases

(c) Pump blood

(d) Digest food

23. Which of the following is the national fruit of India?

(a) 

(b)

(c)

(d)

24. Read statement I and II carefully. Choose the correct answer from given options.

Statement I: Day and night occur due to earth's rotation around sun.

Statement II: Day and night occur due to earth's rotation on its axis.

(a) Only statement I is true.

(b) Only statement II is true.

(c) Both statements are true.

(d) Both statements are false.

25. Which colour of Indian flag symbolizes peace?

(a) White

(b) Blue

(c) Saffron

(d) Green

Name : __________

Number of Questions : 40

Max. Marks : 40

Time : 2 Hours

There is no negative marking in the test.

1. A strip of water having land on two sides is called __________________.
   - (a) lake
   - (b) pond
   - (c) plain
   - (d) desert

2. Who is the current Prime Minister of pakistan?
   - (a) Imran Khan
   - (b) Nawaz Sharif
   - (c) Benazir Bhutto
   - (d) Aamir Khan

3. While travelling in a car, we should wear seat belts because ______________.
   - (a) They save lives.
   - (b) It is a law to wear seat belts.
   - (c) Both A and B
   - (d) None of these

4. Which of the following should we use to cross a road?
   - (a) Zebra crossing
   - (b) Pavements
   - (c) Barricades
   - (d) None of these

5. For how long does each season of the year last?
   - (a) Two months
   - (b) Three months
   - (c) Four months
   - (d) Five months

Space for Rough Work

6. In which season birds migrate to far off places for food and favourable climate?

(a) Summer   (b) Winter

(c) Autumn   (d) Spring

7. Due to which of the following phenomena do seasons happen on earth?

(a) Revolution of earth

(b) Rotation of earth

(c) Revolution of moon

(d) Gravitation of earth

8. In which season some animals hibernate?

(a) Summer   (b) Winter

(c) Autumn   (d) Spring

9. Atal Bihari Vajpayee, who passed away recently, was associated with which political party?

(a) BJP

(b) Congress

(c) AAP

(d) BSP

10. The earth's spin around its axis is called ______________ ____________.

(a) Revolution

(b) Rotation

(c) Polarization

(d) Gravitation

11. If it's day in northern hemisphere, it will be __________ in southern hemisphere.

(a) Day   (b) Summer

(c) Night   (d) Winter

12. Plants use carbon dioxide for ____________.

(a) Movement

(b) Respiration

(c) Excretion

(d) Making Food

13. Why are plants necessary for humans?

(a) They provide food

(b) They provide water

(c) They increase air temperature

(d) None of these

14. Who is the Current Defence Minister of India?

(a) 

(b) 

(c) 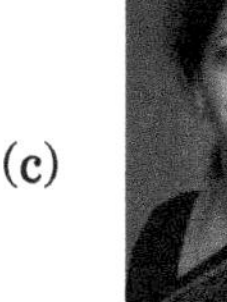

(d) None of these

15. Euro is a common currency in most of the countries in ___________________.

(a) Asia

(b) Europe

(c) North America

(d) South America

16. In which continent, there is no desert?

(a) Asia   (b) Africa

(c) Europe   (d) Australia

17. Which of the following vehicles is specially designed for disabled?

(a) 

(b) 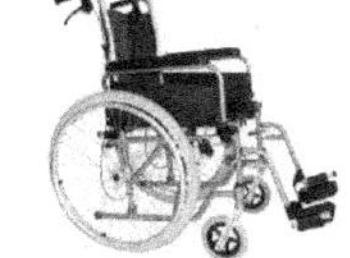

(c) 

(d) 

Space for Rough Work

---

18. Temperature of earth would go up if amount of green-house gases _______________.

(a) Increases

(b) Decreases

(c) Remains constant

(d) None of these

19. Which of the following causes athlete's foot disease?

(a) Fungi   (b) Bacteria

(c) Viruses   (d) Rats

20. Most of water related diseases are caused by _______________.

(a) Jellyfish   (b) Viruses

(c) Bacteria   (d) Crabs

21. Which of the following is the largest organ in human body?

(a) Liver   (b) Lungs

(c) Heart   (d) Brain

22. Our lungs are like _______________.

(a) Sponges   (b) Balloons

(c) Marbles   (d) Whistles

23. Which harmful gas is thrown out of body by respiratory system?

(a) Oxygen

(b) Carbon dioxide

(c) Carbon monoxide

(d) Hydrogen

24. Which of the following nutrients helps in fighting diseases?

(a) Fat

(b) Carbohydrate

(c) Protein

(d) Vitamin

25. Fibrous foods are good for our _______.

(a) Immune system

(b) Digestive system

(c) Growth

(d) Movement

26. Gastric juices are produced in

___________.

(a) Lungs   (b) Liver

(c) Stomach   (d) Mouth

27. There are about ________ bones in an infant's body.

(a) 100   (b) 200

(c) 300   (d) 400

28. Heartbeat in children is __________ adults.

(a) The same as in

(b) Faster than

(c) Slower than

(d) None of these

29. The study of living beings is known as ______________.

(a) Biology   (b) Physics

(c) Ecology   (d) Geography

30. Size of human heart is equal to our _____________.

(a) head   (b) fist

(c) arm   (d) thumb

31. Which is the innermost layer of earth?

(a) Core   (b) Mantle

(c) Lava   (d) Crust

32. How much time does sunlight take to reach earth?

(a) 8 minutes

(b) 8 minutes 20 seconds

(c) 9 minutes

(d) 9 minutes 30 seconds

33. Which of the following is a reason for global warming?

(a) Earth's rotation

(b) Earth's revolution

(c) Earth's gravitation

(d) Earth's pollution

Space for Rough Work

34. Earth is also known as __________

__________.

(a) The blue planet

(b) The black planet

(c) The green planet

(d) The red planet

35. Which colour of Indian national flag indicates courage and strength?

(a) Saffron   (b) White

(c) Blue   (d) Green

36. Which of the following is the national tree of India?

(a) Apple   (b) Mango

(c) Banana   (d) Banyan

37. Which of the following is a grain eating bird with short beak?

(a) Parrot

(b) Crow

(c) Sparrow

(d) Pigeon

38. Read the following statements

I. Every living organism is a part of an ecosystem.

II. Organisms live in an area called habitat.

Choose the correct option.

(a) I is true

(b) II is true

(c) Both I and II are true

(d) Both I and II are false

39. Which of the following planets is known as the morning & evening star?

(a) Mars   (b) Jupiter

(c) Venus   (d) Saturn

40. Your weight on earth is 24 kg. If you go to moon, your weight will __________.

(a) Increase

(b) Decrease

(c) Remain constant

(d) First increase then decrease

Space for Rough Work

OLYMPIAD
Mock Test 4

Name : __________

Number of Questions : 40

Max. Marks : 40

Time : 2 Hours

There is no negative marking in the test.

1. A strip of land having water on two sides is called ______________.
   - (a) Lake
   - (b) River
   - (c) Isthmus
   - (d) Strait

2. In which of the following season do we ski?
   - (a) Summer
   - (b) Winter
   - (c) Autumn
   - (d) Spring

3. The axis of earth is __________.
   - (a) Vertical
   - (b) Curved
   - (c) Tilted
   - (d) Circular

4. Read the following statements.

   I. Animals depend on plants for food.

   II. Plants need sunlight to produce food.

   Choose the correct option.
   - (a) Only I is true
   - (b) Only II is true
   - (c) Both I and II are true.
   - (d) Both I and II are false.

Space for Rough Work

5. We get vitamin C from __________.

(a)
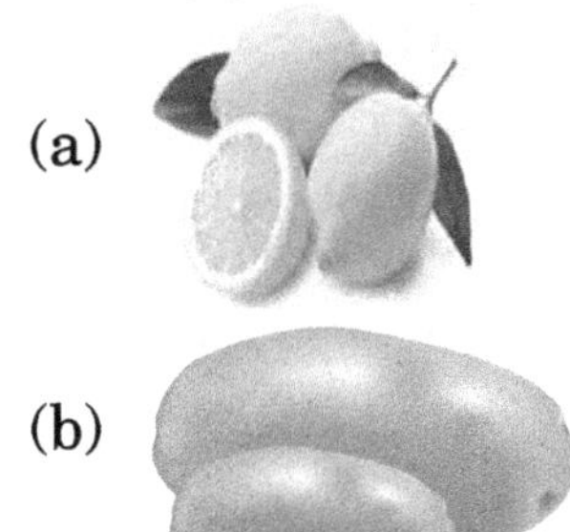

(b)
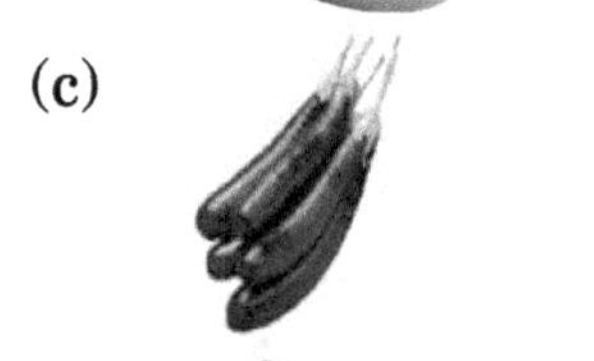

(c)

(d)

6. In which of the following continents, half of the world's diamonds are found?

(a) Asia (b) Europe

(c) Africa (d) Australia

7. The headquarters of companies like Facebook, Google and Apple are situated in __________.

(a) France

(b) Germany

(c) Australia

(d) America (North)

8. In which continent, there are no towns, villages or cities?

(a) Africa (b) Antarctica

(c) Australia (d) Europe

9. Greenhouse effect helps in _____ __________.

(a) Keeping temperature of earth balanced

(b) Keeping rivers clean

(c) Protecting wildlife

(d) Protecting the ozone layer

10. Glaciers would start melting and there would be more floods if greenhouse gases __________.

(a) Increase

(b) Decrease

(c) Remain stable

(d) None of these

11. Which of the following is a green house gas?

(a) Nitrogen

(b) Oxygen

(c) Hydrogen

(d) Carbon dioxide

——————— Space for Rough Work ———————

12. Which of the following insects spreads malaria?

(a) 

(b) 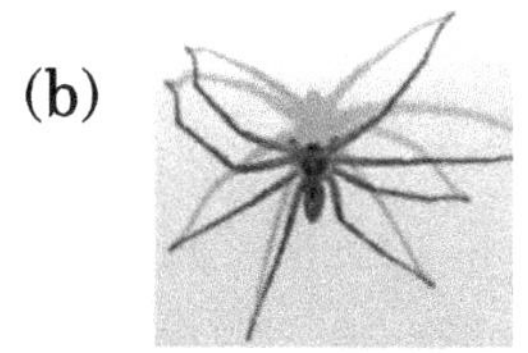

(c) 

(d) 

13. Which of the following is NOT a healthy habit?

(a) Brushing teeth

(b) Washing Hands

(c) Drinking clean water

(d) Eating street food

14. Which of the following is NOT an example of germ?

(a) Fungi   (b) Bacteria

(c) Virus   (d) Cell

15. Which of the following is helpful in digestion process?

(a) Fungi   (b) Bacteria

(c) Virus   (d) Parasite

16. Which of the following has important role in respiration in human body?

(a) Liver   (b) Lung

(c) Stomach   (d) Kidney

17. What is the function of kidneys in human body?

(a) Help in growth of body.

(b) Collect air for respiration.

(c) Remove waste products from body.

(d) Help in digesting food.

18. Sometimes, we cough while eating food if the food enters ___________.

(a) Windpipe   (b) Lungs

(c) Liver   (d) Stomach

19. Which of the following nutrients gives us energy slowly?

(a) Carbohydrate

(b) Fat

(c) Protein

(d) Fiber

20. Which of the following is a rich source of carbohydrate?

(a) 

(b) 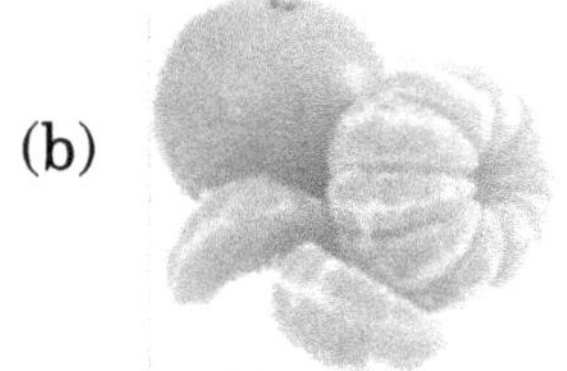

(c) 

(d) 

21. What is the full form of SMS?

(a) Service Mobile System

(b) Short Messaging Service

(c) Speed Message System

(d) Speed Mobile System

22. Saliva is produced in ________ __________.

(a) Mouth   (b) Food pipe

(c) Stomach   (d) Liver

Space for Rough Work

---

23. 50% of our bones are found in our

_____________.

(a) Head

(b) Mouth

(c) Stomach

(d) Hands and feet

24. Bones in our shoulder are also known as _____________.

(a) Neck bones

(b) Pelvic bones

(c) Collar bones

(d) Skull bones

25. Which of the following plays an important role in making our bones stronger?

(a) Salt   (b) Sugar

(c) Vitamin   (d) Calcium

26. Our heart gets oxygen from

_____________.

(a) Lungs   (b) Stomach

(c) Nose   (d) Mouth

27. Teeth not only help you chew food, but they also help you

_____________.

(a) Taste   (b) Talk

(c) Hear   (d) Think

28. Canine type of teeth help in

_____________.

(a) Chewing   (b) Tearing

(c) Cutting   (d) Biting

29. How many milk teeth a small child normally has?

(a) 10   (b) 12

(c) 20   (d) 32

30. Teeth do not help us in _______

__________.

(a) Speaking   (b) Biting

(c) Chewing   (d) Breathing

31. Konark Sun Temple is situated in

_____________.

(a) Andhra Pradesh

(b) Karnataka

(c) Maharashtra

(d) Odisha

Space for Rough Work

32. Who has written the constitution of India?

(a) 

(b) 

(c) 

(d) 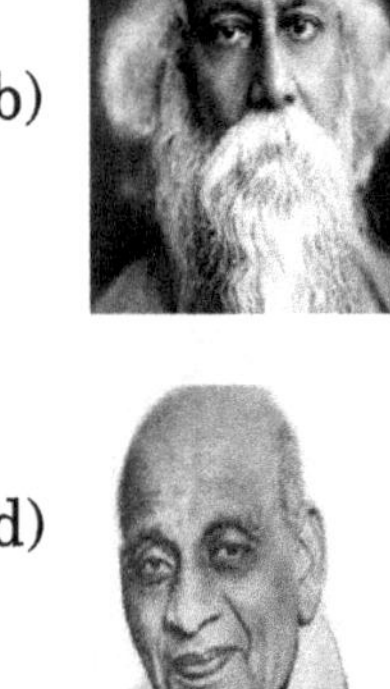

33. Which of the following is known as the national river of India?

(a) Ganga

(b) Yamuna

(c) Brahmputra

(d) Krishna

34. Bodh Gaya in Bihar is related to ___________.

(a) 

(b) 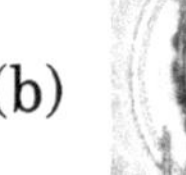

(c) 

(d) 

35. Which of the following is the capital of Jharkhand?

(a) Jamshedpur

(b) Bhopal

(c) Raipur

(d) Ranchi

36. Which of the following is the currency of Australia?

(a) Euro   (b) Dollar

(c) Pound   (d) Franc

37. Which of the following birds makes its nest as shown in the image below?

(a) Crow

(b) Parrot

(c) Weaver Bird

(d) Pigeon

38. Which of the following has a strong curved beak to tear flesh?

(a) Woodpecker

(b) Crane

(c) Pigeon

(d) Eagle

39. Jim Corbett National Park is situated in ____________.

(a) Arunachal Pradesh

(b) Karnataka

(c) Madhya Pradesh

(d) Uttarakhand

40. Which of the following is NOT a component of ecosystem?

(a) Producers

(b) Consumers

(c) Decomposers

(d) Factories

Name : __________

Max. Marks : 40

Number of Questions : 40

Time : 2 Hours

There is no negative marking in the test.

1. Read the following statements.
   I. Sun is not a part of any ecosystem.
   II. Earth is the biggest planet.
   Choose the correct option.
   (a) Only I is true
   (b) Only II is true
   (c) Both I and II are true.
   (d) Both I and II are false.

2. Which is the smallest planet among the following?
   (a) Mars   (b) Saturn
   (c) Earth   (d) Mercury

3. Which part of human body is shown in the image given below?

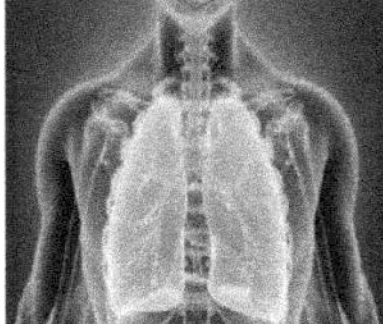

   (a) Kidney   (b) Heart
   (c) Liver   (d) Lungs

4. Which of the following is an aerial animal?
   (a) Sparrow   (b) Zebra
   (c) Bison   (d) Penguin

5. Deficiency of which of the following vitamins causes night blindness?
   (a) Vitamin A   (b) Vitamin B
   (c) Vitamin C   (d) Vitamin D

6. How many liver/s does/do the human body have?
   (a) One   (b) Two
   (c) Three   (d) Four

7. In which country is the animal shown in the image below found?
   (a) Australia
   (b) Brazil
   (c) New Zealand
   (d) South Africa

--- *Space for Rough Work* ---

8. _________ is the capital of China
  (a) Shanghai   (b) Beijing
  (c) Osaka   (d) Hong Kong

9. The image shown below is the national flag of _____________.

  (a) France   (b) USA
  (c) China   (d) UK

10. Who built Qutab Minar at Delhi?
  (a) Akbar
  (b) Bahadur Shah Zafar
  (c) Qutubuddin Aibak
  (d) Humanyun

11. Identify the sportsperson shown in the image below.

  (a) Saina Nehwal
  (b) PV Sindhu
  (c) Sania Mirza
  (d) Mithali Raj

12. Children's Day is celebrated on __________.
  (a) 5th September
  (b) 2nd October
  (c) 14th November
  (d) 10th December

13. One US dollar is equal to approximately ___________.
  (a) 55 rupees   (b) 65 rupees
  (c) 75 rupees   (d) 85 rupees

14. A person who sells medicines is called a _________.
  (a) Physicist   (b) Doctor
  (c) Scientist   (d) Pharmacist

15. What is full form of IPL?
  (a) Indian Petroleum Limited
  (b) Indian Premier League
  (c) Indian Public Library
  (d) Internet Protection Law

16. Kaziranga National Park is in __________.
  (a) Tamil Nadu
  (b) Karnataka
  (c) Assam
  (d) Madhya Pradesh

Space for Rough Work

17. How many states are there in India?
    (a) 26 (b) 27
    (c) 28 (d) 29

18. Asthma is a disease of _________ __________.
    (a) Ears (b) Lungs
    (c) Eyes (d) Heart

19. How many players are there in a football team?
    (a) 6 (b) 8
    (c) 9 (d) 11

20. Which of the following is made from fruits?
    (a) Ghee (b) Honey
    (c) Jam (d) Butter

21. Which of the following is different from the other three?
    (a) School (b) Teacher
    (c) Student (d) Principal

22. A figure with 4 sides is called a _______________.
    (a) Circle (b) Triangle
    (c) Rectangle (d) Pentagon

23. Delhi is situated on the bank of river _________________.
    (a) Ganga (b) Yamuna
    (c) Narmada (d) Gomti

24. A place where birds are kept is called _______________.
    (a) Aviary (b) Aquarium
    (c) Park (d) Zoo

25. How many seconds are there in an hour?
    (a) 60 (b) 180
    (c) 360 (d) 3600

26. Butter and ghee are rich in __________.
    (a) Carbohydrate
    (b) Protein
    (c) Fat
    (d) Vitamin

27. Which of the following nutrients provides instant energy?
    (a) Glucose (b) Butter
    (c) Egg (d) Potato

28. Most of the harmful bacteria present in food are killed in __________.
    (a) Mouth (b) Stomach
    (c) Liver (d) Kidney

Space for Rough Work

29. The outermost layer of tooth is called _________________.

    (a) Enamel   (b) Pulp

    (c) Skin   (d) Root

30. Identify the monument shown in the image given below?

    (a) Jantar Mantar

    (b) Hawa Mahal

    (c) Red Fort

    (d) Victoria Memorial

31. Read the statements given below carefully and choose the right answer.

    Statement I: Baby of an elephant is called calf.

    Statement II: Baby of a dog is called puppy.

    (a) Only statement I is correct

    (b) Only statement II is correct

    (c) Both statements I and II are correct

    (d) Both statements I and II are wrong

32. Match states with their capitals and choose the correct answer from given options.

	States		Capitals
1.	Manipur	(a)	Bhopal
2.	Chhatisgarh	(b)	Bengaluru
3.	Madhya Pradesh	(c)	Imphal
4.	Karnataka	(d)	Raipur

    (a) 1-a, 2-c, 3-d, 4-b

    (b) 1-d, 2-a, 3-b, 4-c

    (c) 1-c, 2-d, 3-a, 4-b

    (d) 1-b, 2-c, 3-d, 4-a

33. Which of the following planets is farthest from the sun?

    (a) Mars   (b) Jupiter

    (c) Uranus   (d) Neptune

——————————— *Space for Rough Work* ———————————

34. Who was the first Governor General of independent India?

    (a) Bal Gangadhar Tilak

    (b) C. Rajagopalachari

    (c) Lala Lajpat Rai

    (d) Vallabhbhai Patel

35. Which of the following is an aquatic plant?

    (a) Hydrilla

    (b) Watermelon

    (c) Mint

    (d) Rose

36. Which of the following parts of a plant grows into a fruit?

    (a) Root   (b) Stem

    (c) Leaf   (d) Flower

37. Which of the following cities is known as 'The Golden City'?

    (a) Jodhpur   (b) Amritsar

    (c) Allahabad   (d) Bengaluru

38. 'Bharatnatyam' dance is associated with ______.

    (a) Tamil Nadu   (b) Karnataka

    (c) Kerala   (d) Maharshtra

39. Which of the following movies won National Film Award 2017 for best film in Hindi?

    (a) Neerja   (b) Airlift

    (c) Dear Zindagi (d) Sarbjit

40. 'Eiffel Tower' is located in ______.

    (a) London

    (b) Paris

    (c) New York

    (d) Washington

LOGICAL REASONING MOCK TEST 1–5

OLYMPIAD
Mock Test 1

Name : __________

Number of Questions : 30

There is no negative marking in the test.

Max. Marks : 30

Time : 1 Hour 30 Minutes

1. Find the odd one out.

(a) 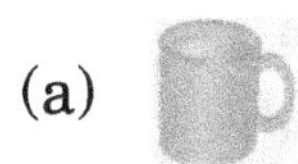 (b) 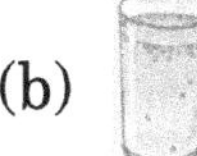

(c)  (d) 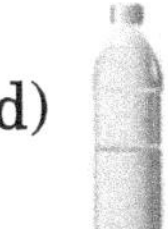

2. Find the matching pair.

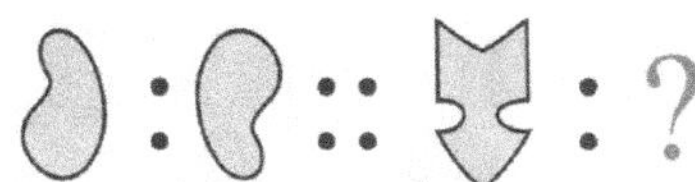

(a)  (b) 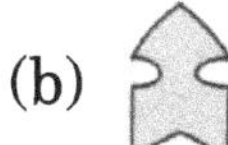

(c) 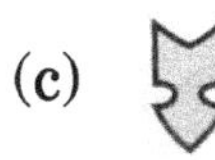 (d) 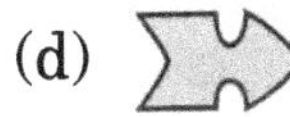

3. Find the missing number in the given pattern.

21, 31, 41, 51, ___?____

(a) 61 (b) 71

(c) 60 (d) 81

4. Which is the longest stick?

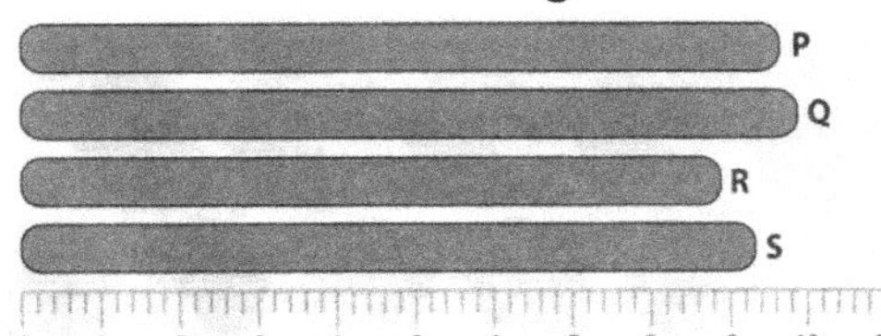

(a) S (b) P

(c) R (d) Q

Space for Rough Work

5. The figure has _______ straight lines.

   (a) 11   (b) 12

   (c) 13   (d) 14

6. In which larger shape is the shape hidden?

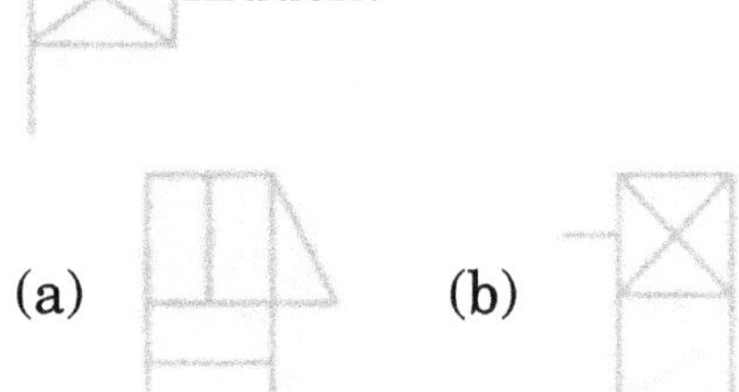

   (a)   (b)

   (c)   (d)

7. Which balloon is fifth to the right of balloon D?

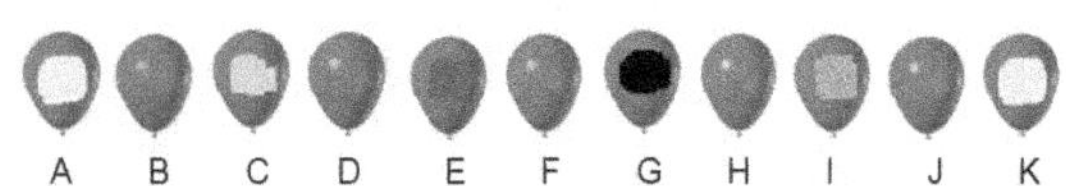

   (a) E   (b) I

   (c) J   (d) F

8. If 'white' is called 'black', 'black' is called 'blue', 'blue' is called 'yellow', then colour of milk is _________ .

   (a) black   (b) white

   (c) blue   (d) yellow

9. There are 4 cars and 2 scooters in a parking lot. How many wheels do they have in all?

   (a) 18   (b) 19

   (c) 20   (d) 22

DIRECTIONS (Qs. 10 & 11): Observe the picture carefully and answer the following questions.

10. How many items are there in the picture?

   (a) 16   (b) 10

   (c) 8   (d) 14

11. How many items are there between pen and alarm?

   (a) 8   (b) 9

   (c) 14   (d) 15

12. Arrange the given pictures in the proper sequence by using their alphabets.

A

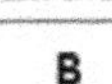

B

C

D

   (a) CDBA   (b) DCBA

   (c) BCDA   (d) ADBC

13. ...?..

   (a)    (b)

   (c)   (d)

14. The figure is made up of _________ triangles.

   (a) 4   (b) 5
   (c) 6   (d) 7

15. Find the odd one out.
   (a) AC   (b) BD
   (c) DF   (d) FG

16. Which toy costs the most?

   (a) P   (b) Q
   (c) R   (d) S

Space for Rough Work

17. Find the odd one out.

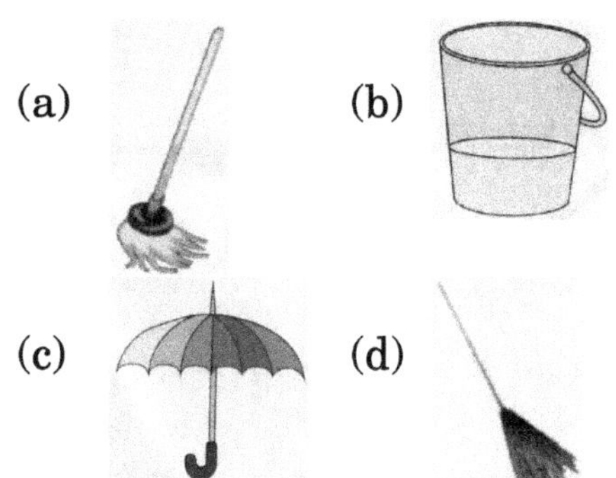

(a)   (b)

(c)   (d)

18. What comes next in the series given?

(a)   (b)

(c)   (d)

19. 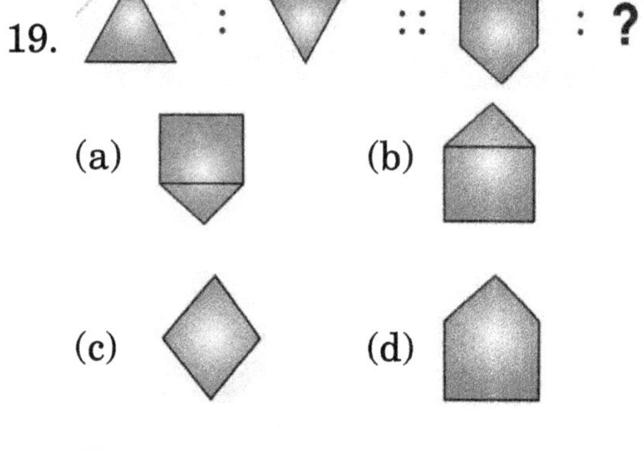

(a)   (b)

(c)   (d)

20. How many groups of 5 apples (If there are 4 apples in each plate) can be formed from these apples?

(a) 4   (b) 3

(c) 5   (d) 2

21. Kavya ranks tenth from the top and fourth from the bottom in a class. How many students are there in the class?

(a) 6   (b) 8

(c) 12   (d) 13

Space for Rough Work

22. In a certain language, MAN is coded as OBP, then how is SUN coded?

    (a) TVO   (b) NUS

    (c) UVP   (d) TUO

23. Observe the figure carefully and answer the question based on it.

Which shape is embedded in the above figure?

(a)    (b) 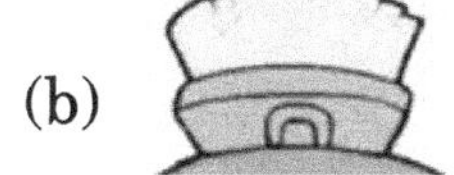

(c) 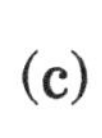   (d) 

24. Who is the tallest and shortest among them?

    (a) Piju and Hojo

    (b) Lova and Mio

    (c) Mio and Gina

    (d) Gina and Lova

DIRECTIONS (Qs. 25 to 27): Read the following information carefully and answer the questions based on it.

Kaka is shorter than Ana but taller than Mahi. Nanu is shorter than Mahi.

25. Who is tallest among them?

    (a) Ana   (b) Mahi

    (c) Nanu   (d) Kaka

26. Who is between Kaka and Nanu?

   (a) Ana

   (b) Mahi

   (c) Both

   (d) None of these

27. Who is shortest among them?

   (a) Mahi

   (b) Kaka

   (c) Nanu

   (d) Ana

28. Arrange the given pictures in the proper sequence by using their alphabets.

   (a) PQSR

   (b) PSRQ

   (c) RSPQ

   (d) QRSP

29. Beaker _______ contains the most amount of water.

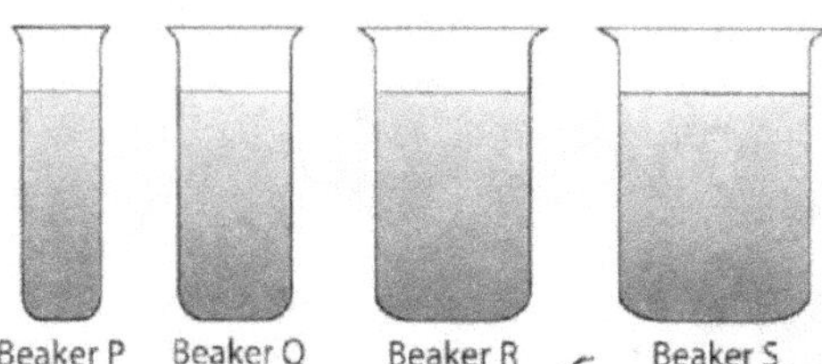

   (a) Q

   (b) R

   (c) P

   (d) S

30. What comes next in the series given?

   (a) 15

   (b) 17

   (c) 19

   (d) 20

Space for Rough Work

OLYMPIAD
Mock Test
2

Name : ___________

Number of Questions : 30

There is no negative marking in the test.

Max. Marks : 30

Time : 1 Hour 30 Minutes

1. Find the next term.

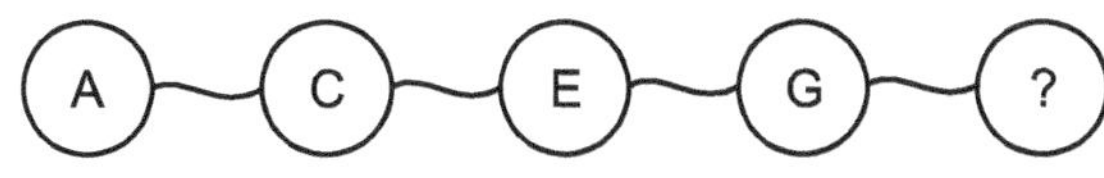

   (a) H   (b) I

   (c) J   (d) None of these

2. The figure is made up of __________ squares.

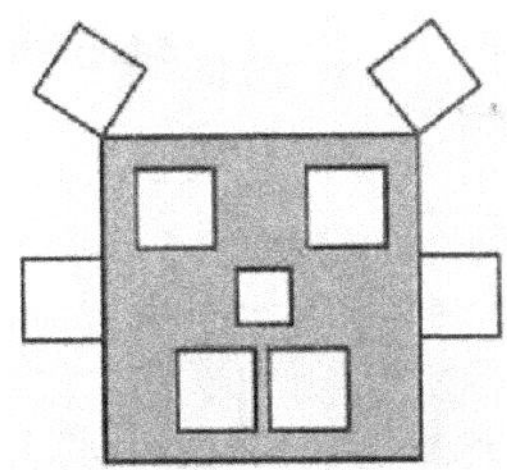

   (a) 7   (b) 8

   (c) 9   (d) 10

3. Find the odd one out.

   (a)    (b) 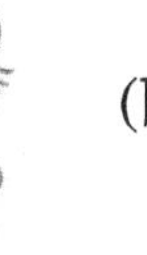

   (c)    (d) 

DIRECTIONS (Qs. 4 to 6): Observe the given figure carefully and answer the questions below.

Space for Rough Work

---

4. Which ant is fifth from left end?

   (a) P   (b) E

   (c) C   (d) K

5. Ant__________ is fourth to the right of ant M.

   (a) J   (b) C

   (c) D   (d) E

6. If Ant R and E interchange their positions, then Ant_____ is at left end.

   (a) R   (b) E

   (c) J   (d) K

7. How many triangles are there in the given figure?

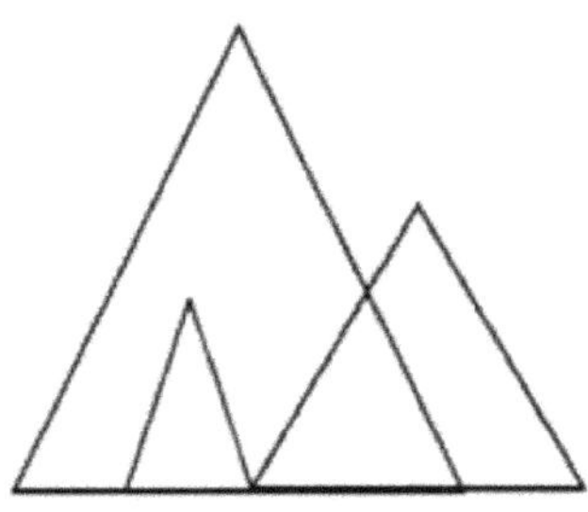

   (a) 3   (b) 4

   (c) 5   (d) 7

8. Who is shortest among them?

   (a) G   (b) A

   (c) D   (d) I

9. If MANGO is written as MAOGN, then CAMEL will be written as_____.

   (a) LEMAC   (b) ACLME

   (c) CALEM   (d) MELCA

10. If Nose is called Hand, Hand is called Hair, Hair is called Eyes, Eyes is called Fingers, Then fingers is a part of_____?

   (a) Eyes   (b) Nose

   (c) Hand   (d) Hairs

DIRECTIONS (Qs. 11 to 13): Observe the picture of a garden and answer the following questions.

11. How many children are there in the garden?

    (a) 4   (b) 2

    (c) 5   (d) 0

12. How many animals are there in the garden?

    (a) 5   (b) 6

    (c) 2   (d) 1

13. In the picture how many birds are flying in the sky?

    (a) 1   (b) 2

    (c) 3   (d) 0

14. Observe the figure carefully and the answer the question based on it.

Which shape is embedded is the above figure?

(a)    (b) 

(c)    (d) 

15. Which statement will make this equation complete?

45 _________ 20

    (a) is smaller than

    (b) is greater than

    (c) is equal to

    (d) none of these

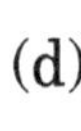

Space for Rough Work

16. The month whose name begins with _____ is the 4th month of the year. It has _____ days in a month.

    (a) A, 31   (b) A, 30

    (c) D, 30   (d) M, 31

17. Estimate 2300 m to kilometre?

    $$2300 \text{ m} = ?$$

    (a) 4 km 300 m (b) 7 km 200 m

    (c) 1 km 300 m (d) 2 km 300 m

18. Which table is heavier than all?

    (a)    (b) 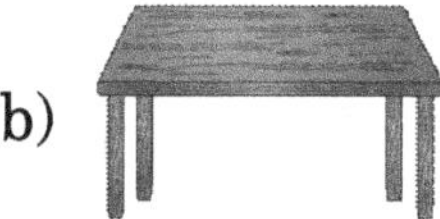

    (c)    (d)

19. Find the odd one out.

    (a) 24   (b) 600

    (c) 71   (c) 15

20. Sunny started his Math exam practice on 5th January. If he practices for 15 days then his practice will finishes on___?

    (a) 18th   (b) 20th

    (c) 19th   (d) 24th

DIRECTIONS (Qs. 21 to 25): Read the information carefully and answer the given questions

P, Q, R and S are sitting on a bench. P is sitting to the next to Q, S is sitting next to R. R is on the third position from left.

Space for Rough Work

21. Who is sitting at the right corner?

    (a) P   (b) Q

    (c) R   (d) S

22. Who is sitting at the second position from right?

    (a) P   (b) Q

    (c) S   (d) R

23. Which two persons are sitting in the middle?

    (a) QP   (b) QS

    (c) PR   (d) PS

24. Who is sitting at the left corner?

    (a) R   (b) P

    (c) S   (d) Q

25. Who is sitting at the second place from left?

    (a) Q   (b) P

    (c) R   (d) S

26. How many stairs are there between 5th stair and 12th stair?

    (a) 7   (b) 8

    (c) 4   (d) 6

27. Arrange the given pictures in the proper sequence by using their alphabets.

    (a) ABCDE   (b) ECDBA

    (c) BEDCA   (d) ACDEB

28. Find the missing number in the given pattern.

    (a) 20   (b) 21

    (c) 23   (d) 25

Space for Rough Work

29. How many circles are there in the figure?

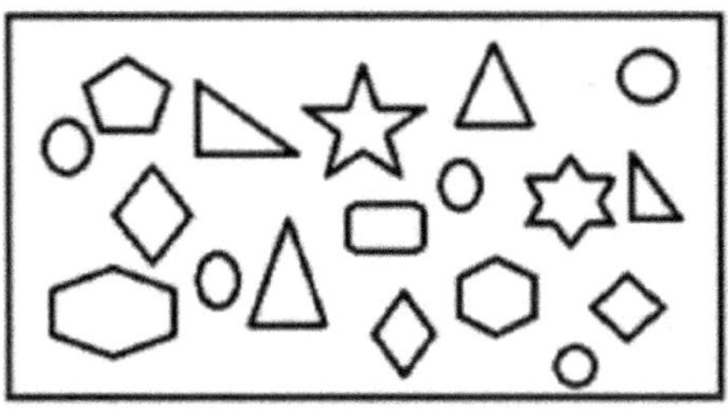

    (a) 4   (b) 5

    (c) 7   (d) 10

30. Estimate the weight of scooter.

    (a) 20-30 kg   (b) 30-50 kg

    (c) 400-570 kg (d) 100-120 kg

Name : __________

Number of Questions : 30

Max. Marks : 30

Time : 1 Hour 30 Minutes

There is no negative marking in the test.

1. If 'chair' is called 'table', 'table is called 'desk' and 'desk' is called 'ladder', then what does a person sit on?

   (a) chair   (b) table

   (c) desk   (d) ladder

2. What comes next in the series given?

   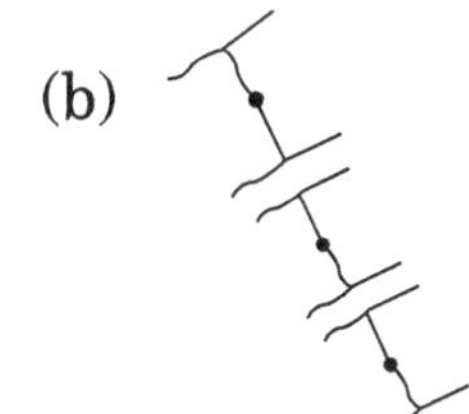

   (a)   (b)

   (c)   (d)

3. Study the given figure.

   How many more circles than rectangles are there?

   (a) 1   (b) 2

   (c) 3   (d) 4

———— Space for Rough Work ————

4. In which larger shapes is the small shape hidden?

(a) 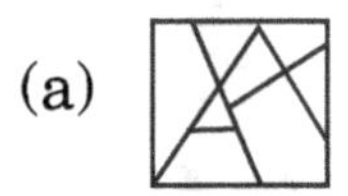   (b) 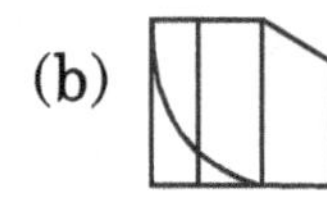

(c) 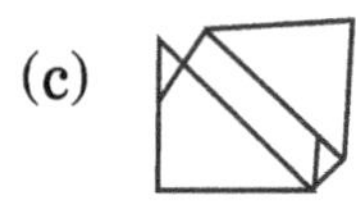   (d) 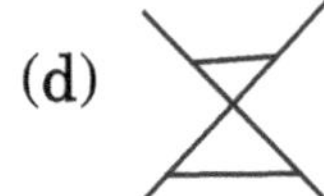

5. Study the number patterns. Fill in the missing numbers in empty row.

8	7	6	5
7	6	5	4
6	5	4	3
?			

(a) 6789   (b) 2345

(c) 1234   (d) 5432

DIRECTIONS (Qs. 6 to 8): Study the given information and answer the following questions.

Anil, Bunny, Chetan and Divansh are sitting on a bench. Anil is sitting next to Bunny. Divansh sitting next to Chetan is on the third position from left.

6. Who is sitting at the right corner?
   (a) Bunny   (b) Anil
   (c) Chetan   (d) Divansh

7. Which two boys are sitting in the middle?
   (a) Bunny, Anil
   (b) Bunny, Divansh
   (c) Anil, Chetan
   (d) Anil, Divansh

8. Who is sitting at the second from left?
   (a) Anil   (b) Chetan
   (c) Divansh   (d) Bunny

9. Find the odd one out.
   (a) 232   (b) 464
   (c) 899   (d) 727

10. Find the odd one out.

(a) 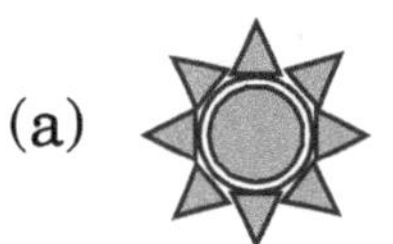   (b) 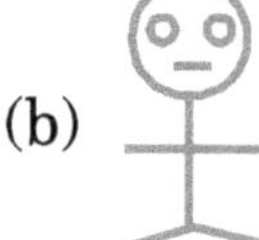

(c) 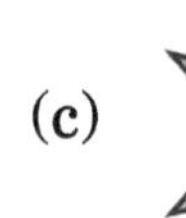   (d) 

11. Find the matching pair.

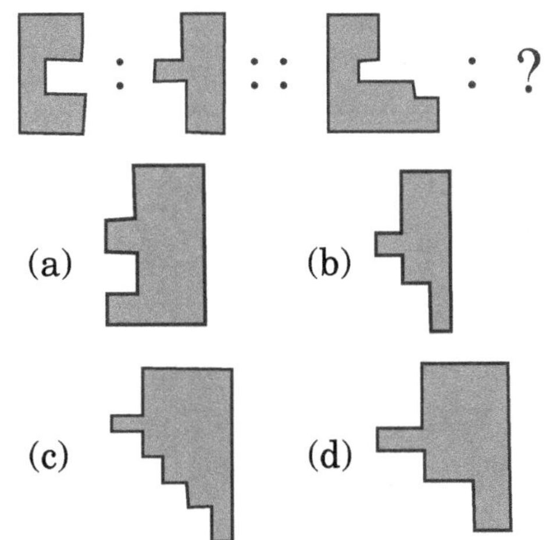

DIRECTIONS (Qs. 12 to 16): Observe the given figure carefully and answer the questions below :

12. Which soldier is third to the left of Soldier C?

(a) B   (b) D

(c) H   (d) A

13. Soldier _______ is third to the left of Soldier A.

(a) B   (b) H

(c) G   (d) C

14. Soldier _______ is fifth to the left of second soldier.

(a) D   (b) H

(c) B   (d) A

15. Soldier _______ is fourth from end.

(a) B   (b) G

(c) H   (d) F

16. Soldier _______ is third to the right of Soldier B.

(a) C   (b) E

(c) G   (d) E

_______________ *Space for Rough Work* _______________

17. Identify the group of 4 sevens.

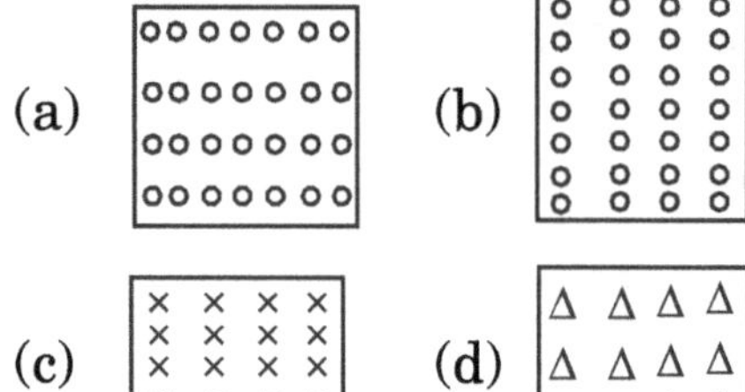

(a)　　　　　　　　(b)

(c)　　　　　　　　(d)

18. Which of the following pair of shapes do not seem to fit together?

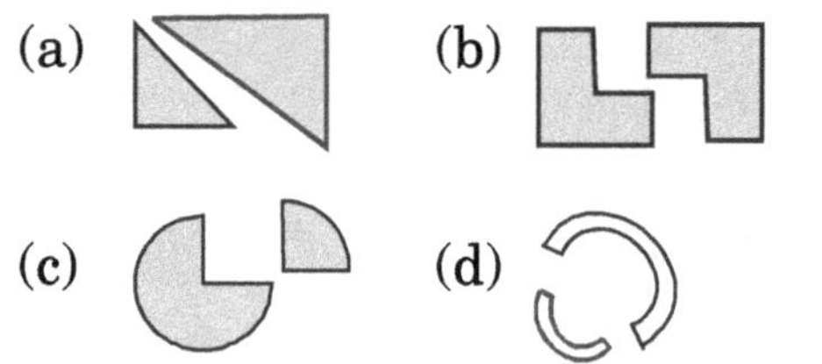

(a)　　　　　　　　(b)

(c)　　　　　　　　(d)

19. String _______ is the shortest and string _______ is the longest.

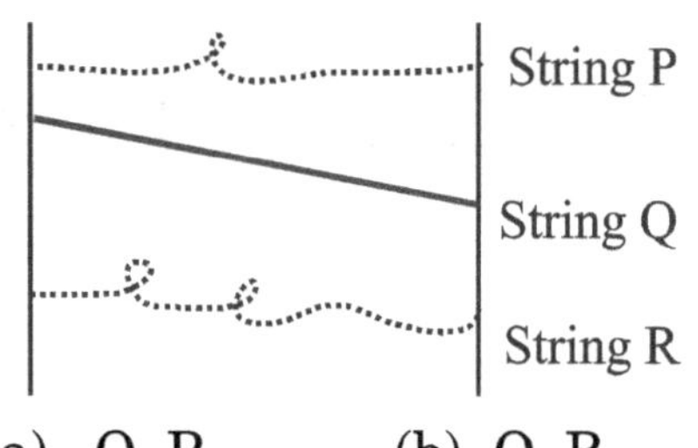

(a)　Q, P　　　　　(b)　Q, R

(c)　P, R　　　　　(d)　R, Q

20. In the question below, there is a relationship between the numbers in the first and second rows. Find the missing number.

First Row　　　　: 2　3　4　5

Second Row　　　: 6　?　12　15

(a)　6　　　　　　(b)　9

(c)　10　　　　　　(d)　5

DIRECTIONS (Qs. 21): Which of the following replaces the question mark (?) so that figure series is formed?

21. 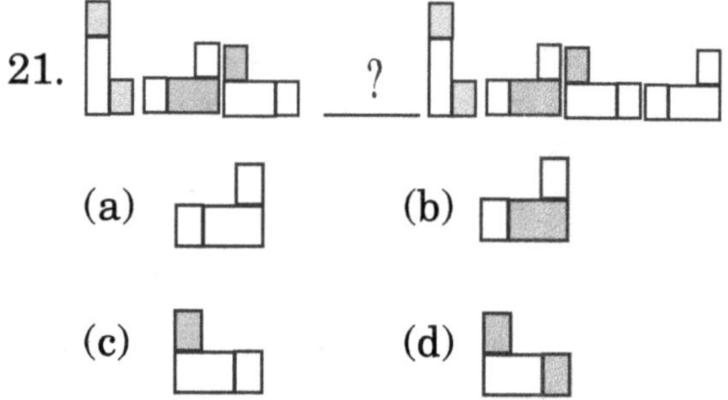

(a)　　　　　　　　(b)

(c)　　　　　　　　(d)

22. Choose the correct order of letters so that is formed we can see the correct word.

　　　　　1 2 3 4 5
　　　　　C A S E L

(a)　3, 1, 5, 2, 4　(b)　3, 1, 2, 5, 4

(c)　4, 5, 1, 3, 2　(d)　1, 2, 3, 4, 5

23. In a certain language, TUB is coded as VWD, then how is CUP coded in that language?

(a) DAQ   (b) PUC

(c) EWR   (d) EUR

DIRECTIONS (Qs. 24 to 27): Observe the picture carefully and give answer the following questions.

Here, R–Red, Y–Yellow, O–Orange, G–Green, P–Purple.

24. How many fruits are there in the picture?

(a) 9   (b) 10

(c) 11   (d) 12

25. How many red-coloured fruits are there in the picture?

(a) 3   (b) 2

(c) 1   (d) 0

26. How many green-coloured fruits are there in the picture?

(a) 1   (b) 3

(c) 2   (d) 4

27. How many fruits are there in between pineapple and apple?

(a) 5   (b) 8

(c) 6   (d) 7

28. Who is shortest among them?

(a) 2   (b) 6

(c) 8   (d) 10

———————— Space for Rough Work ————————

29. Which statement will make this equation complete?

    30 _______ 15 ______ 27

    (a) < and >

    (b) < and <

    (c) > and >

    (d) > and <

30. The figure is made up of _______ circles.

    (a) 5   (b) 7

    (c) 6   (d) 9

———— Space for Rough Work ————

OLYMPIAD
Mock Test 4

Name : __________

Number of Questions : 25

There is no negative marking in the test.

Max. Marks : 25

Time : 1 Hour 30 Minutes

Reasoning

DIRECTION (Q. 1) : Which of the following replaces the questions mark(?) in given number pattern?

1.

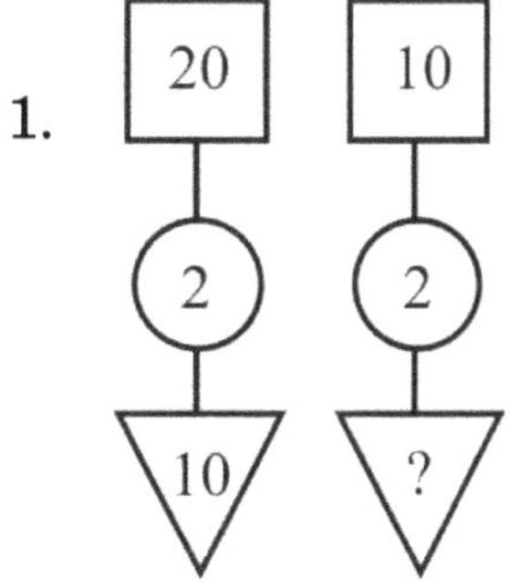

(a) 5   (b) 6

(c) 8   (d) 10

DIRECTION (Q. 2) : Which of the following replaces the question mark (?) so that figure series is formed?

2.

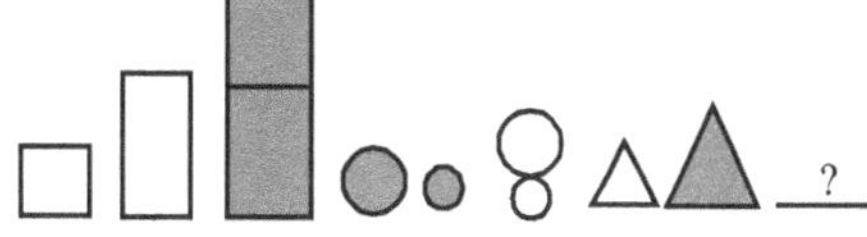

(a) ⟨triangle⟩   (b) ⟨triangle⟩

(c) ⟨triangle⟩   (d) ⟨triangle⟩

3. How many teddy bears will be there in Pattern 5?

_______ Space for Rough Work _______

(a) 11 (b) 12

(c) 9 (d) 14

4. Which is the next number?

2 4 1 3 2 2 1 2 4 1 3 2 2 1 2 4 1 3 2 2 1 2 4 1 ?

(a) 1 (b) 2

(c) 3 (d) 4

5. Box _____ is the heaviest and Box _____ is the lightest.

(a) Z, W (b) Z, X

(c) X, W (d) Z, Y

6. 

_______ kettles () of water will full up 5 such pails.

(a) 20 (b) 25

(c) 15 (d) 22

7. There are _____ triangles in the figure.

(a) 2 (b) 3

(c) 4 (d) 5

8. The figure is made up of _______ squares, ________ circles, ______ rectangles and ________ triangles.

(a) 3, 10, 2, 2 (b) 2, 11, 3, 1

(c) 2, 10, 3, 2 (d) 3, 11, 3, 2

9. (a) 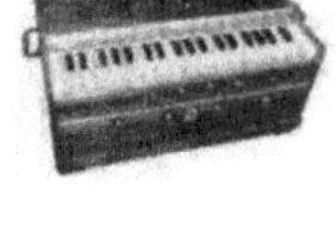 (b) 

(c)  (d)

Space for Rough Work

DIRECTIONS (Qs. 9 & 10): Find the odd one out.

10. (a) 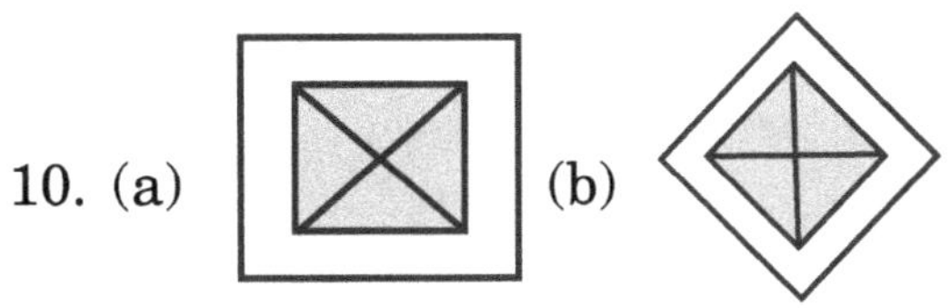 (b)

   (c) 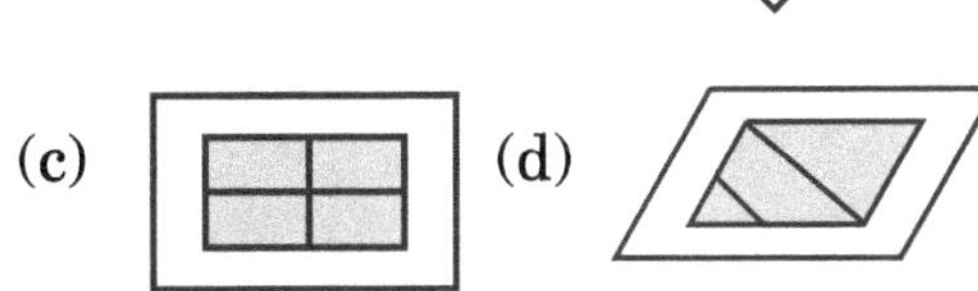 (d)

11. There is a certain relationship between the pair of figure on the either side of : :. Identify the relation between the pair and find the missing figure.

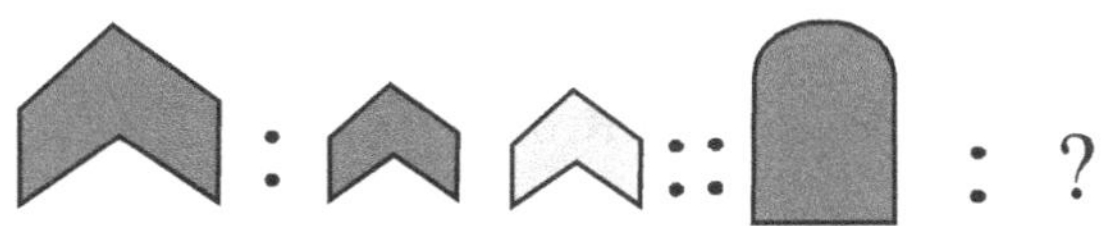 : ?

  (a) 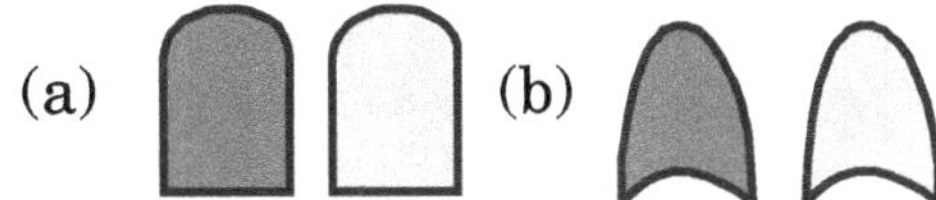 (b)

  (c) 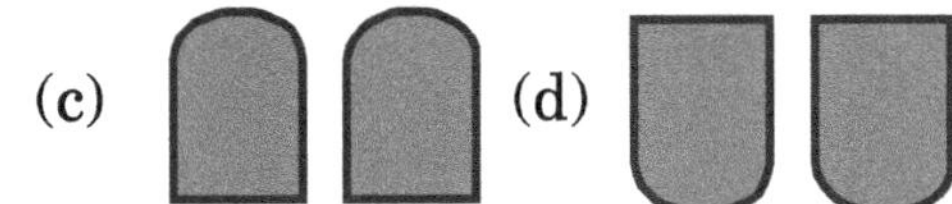 (d)

DIRECTIONS (Qs. 12 to 15): Observe the given figure carefully and answer the questions below.

12. Which bear is fourth from end?

   (a) A   (b) F

   (c) C   (d) G

13. Bear _______ is third to the right of Bear A.

   (a) B   (b) E

   (c) D   (d) G

14. If Bear C and A interchange their positions, then Bear _____ is at right end.

   (a) F   (b) D

   (c) A   (d) G

15. Bear ______ is third from the right end.

   (a) B   (b) A

   (c) G   (d) F

Space for Rough Work

16. Identify the group of 4 triangles (X).

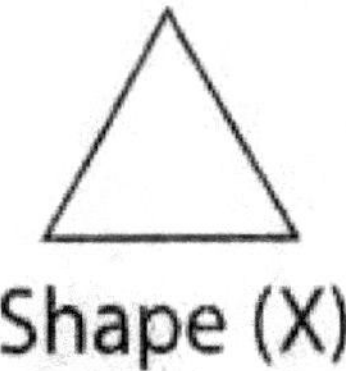

Shape (X)

Group (P)

Group (Q)

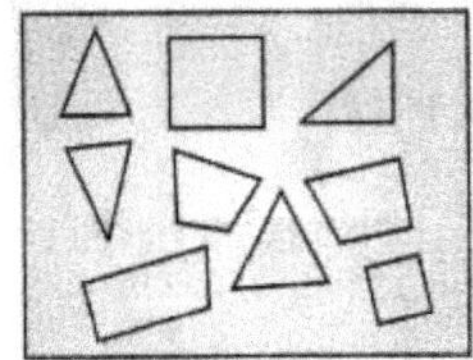

Group (R)

Group (S)

(a) Only P

(b) Only Q

(c) Both P and Q

(d) Both P and S

17. Anjali has some cherries as shown below.

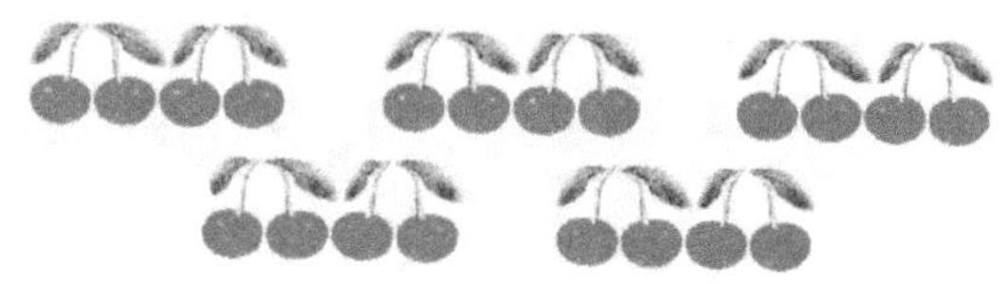

How many cherries are there in each group, if 4 groups having same number of cherries are formed?

(a) 16   (b) 20

(c) 5   (d) 15

18. If 'lion' is called 'rabbit', 'rabbit', is called 'snake', 'snake' is called 'monkey', then the king of jungles is _______.

(a) lion   (b) rabbit

(c) snake   (d) monkey

19. In which larger shapes is the shape  hidden?

(a) 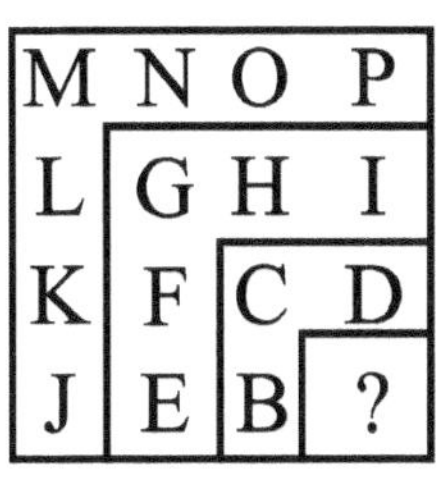

(b)

(c)

(d)

(a) A, B, C, D, E

(b) E, B, C, D, A

(c) C, E, B, D, A

(d) C, E, B, A, D

DIRECTIONS (Qs. 22 & 23): Observe the picture and answer the following questions.

20. Find the alphabet in place of question mark.

M	N	O	P
L	G	H	I
K	F	C	D
J	E	B	?

(a) C (b) F

(c) Z (d) A

21. Arrange the given pictures in the proper sequence by seeing their alphabets.

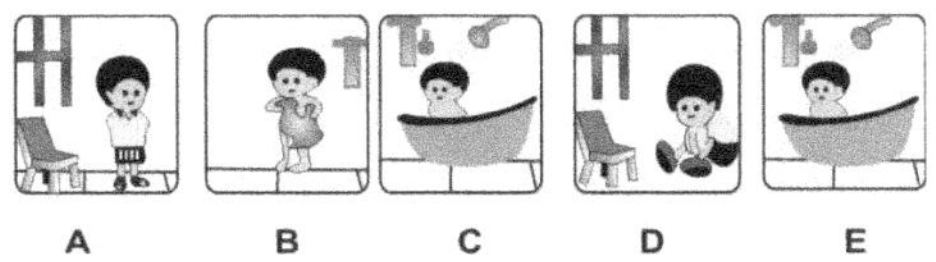

22. How many balloons are there in this picture?

(a) 3 (b) 4

(c) 2 (d) 1

23. How many candles are there on the cake in the picture?

(a) 3 (b) 4

(c) 5 (d) 6

DIRECTIONS (Qs. 24 & 25): Study the information carefully to answer the questions.

Shalu is shorter than Avika but taller than Pari. Nikita is shorter than Pari.

24. Who is shorter among them?

    (a) Shalu   (b) Pari

    (d) Avika   (d) Nikita

25. Who is tallest among them?

    (a) Nikita

    (b) Avika

    (c) Pari

    (d) Shalu

OLYMPIAD
Mock Test 5

Name : __________

Number of Questions : 25

Max. Marks : 25

Time : 1 Hour 30 Minutes

There is no negative marking in the test.

1. Which of the following replaces the question mark (?) in given number pattern?

   (a) 14

   (b) 33

   (c) 20

   (d) 35

2. Which of the following replaces the question mark(?) so that figure series is formed?

   (a)

   (b)

   (c)

   (d)

3. How many flowers will be there in Pattern 4?

   Pattern 1   Pattern 2   Pattern 3

   (a) 10

   (b) 14

   (c) 12

   (d) 16

4. Which is the next alphabet?

   A B C B D D A B C B D D A B C B

   D D A ?

   (a) A

   (b) B

   (c) C

   (d) D

Space for Rough Work

5. How many W are needed to balance 1 Y ?

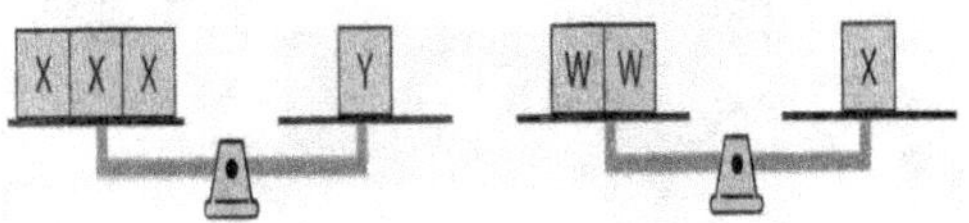

(a) 6

(b) 4

(c) 2

(d) 3

6. Meenu walks from X to Y. Lisa walks from S to T. _______ walks the shorter distance.

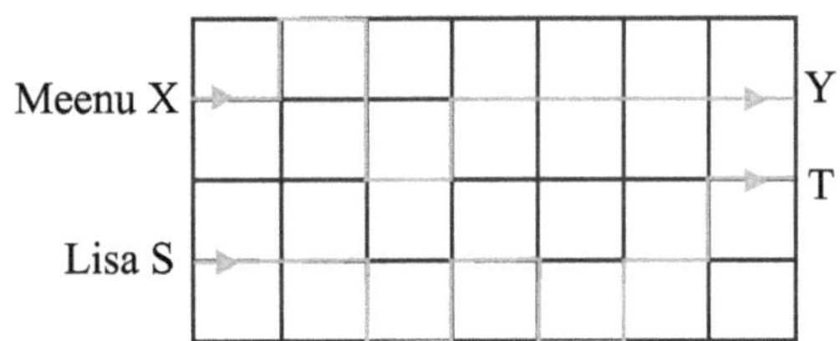

(a) Lisa

(b) Meenu

(c) Both walked the same distance

(d) Can't be determined

7. The figure is made up of _______ triangles and _______ circles.

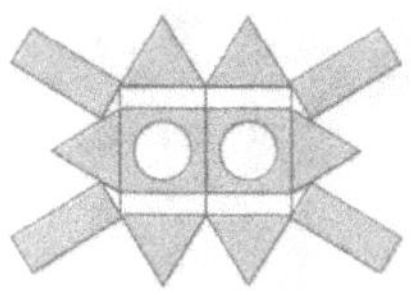

(a) 2, 9

(b) 10, 2

(c) 6, 2

(d) 2, 7

8. There are _______ more triangles than the circles in the given figure.

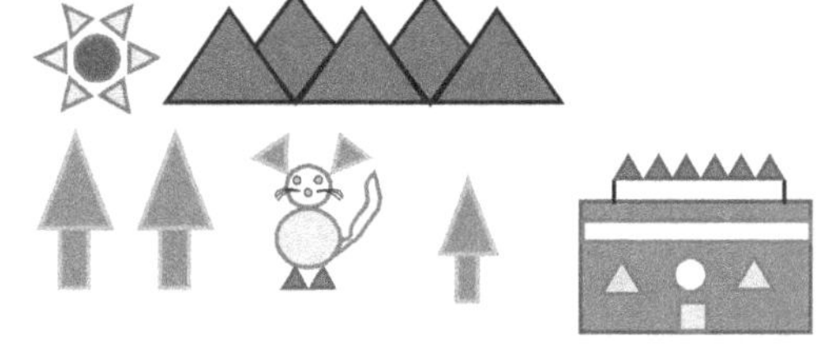

(a) 24

(b) 15

(c) 19

(d) 17

DIRECTIONS (Qs. 9 & 10): Find the odd one out.

9. (a) 

(b) 

(c) 

(d) 

10. (a)    (b) 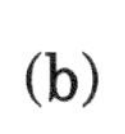

   (c)    (d) 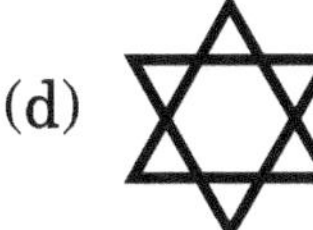

11. There is a certain relationship between figure I & III and II & IV. Identify the relationship and find the missing figure.

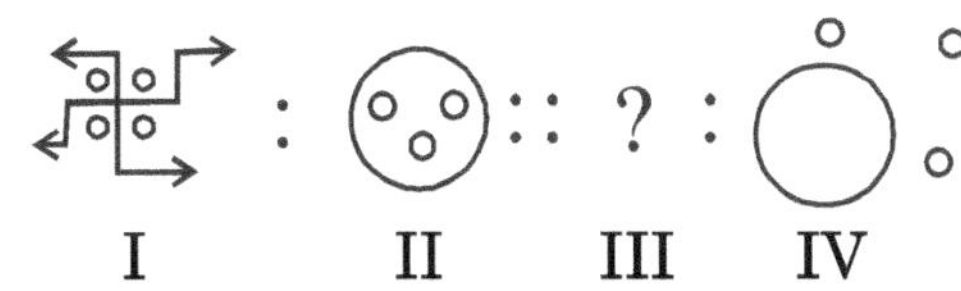

    I   II   III   IV

(a) 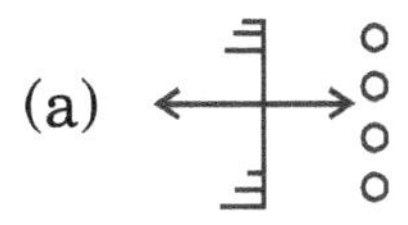   (b) 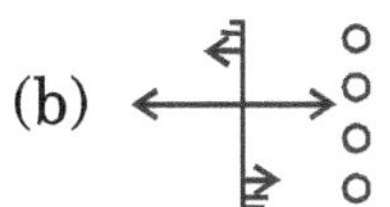

(c) 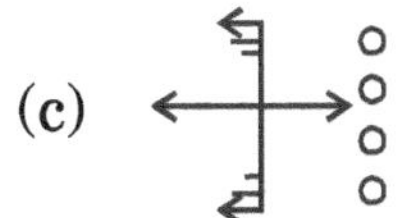   (d) 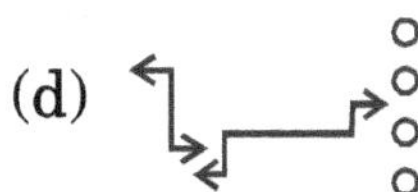

DIRECTIONS (Qs. 12 to 15): Observe the given figure carefully and answer the questions below.

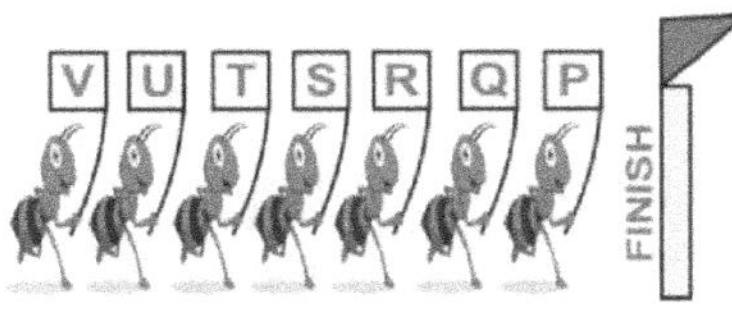

12. Bug _____ is at the third position.

    (a) P   (b) Q

    (c) R   (d) S

13. Bug ______ is at the second position.

    (a) P   (b) Q

    (c) R   (d) S

14. Bug _____ is last from the finish line.

    (a) V   (b) U

    (c) T   (d) S

15. Bug ______ is at the fourth position.

    (a) P   (b) Q

    (c) R   (d) S

Space for Rough Work

16. How many groups of 2 triangles can be formed by triangles given in box?

    (a) 14   (b) 10

    (c) 7   (d) 5

17. How many groups of 4 mangoes can be formed from given fruits?

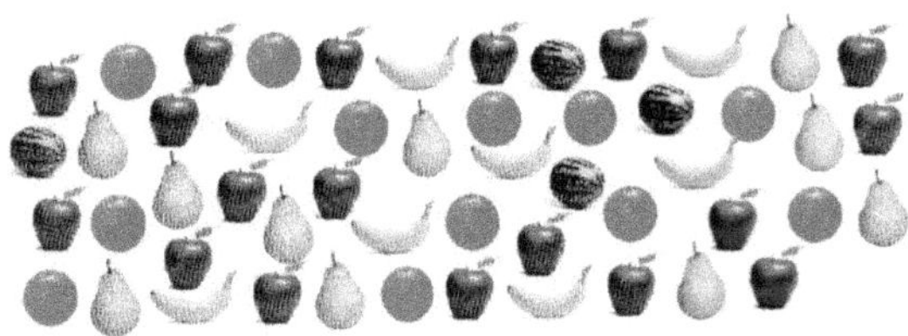

    (a) 2   (b) 4

    (c) 3   (d) 0

18. If 'Sunday' is called 'Monday', 'Monday' is called 'Tuesday', 'Tuesday' is called 'Wednesday', then which of these is called the second day of week?

    (a) Sunday   (b) Monday

    (c) Tuesday   (d) Wednesday

19. In which larger shape is the shape hidden?

    (a) 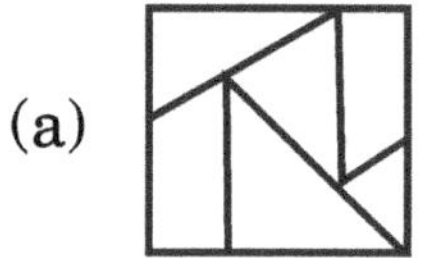   (b) 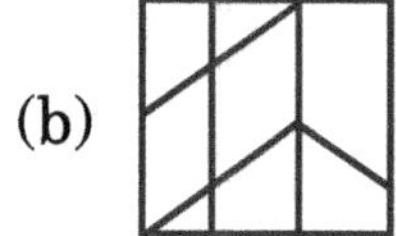

    (c) 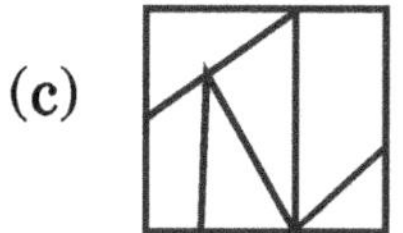   (d) 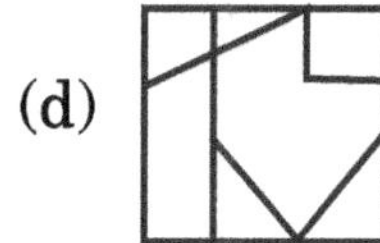

20. Find the alphabet in place of question mark.

N	O	P	Q
M	X	Y	R
L	W	?	S
K	V	U	T

    (a) M   (b) A

    (c) E   (d) Z

DIRECTIONS (Qs. 21 & 22): Study the information carefully and answer the following questions.

The following pictures illustrate the schedule of Mahi's dresses. She starts with Frock at 10 am and rotates the wheel by one step in anticlockwise direction to find the dress for the next hour.

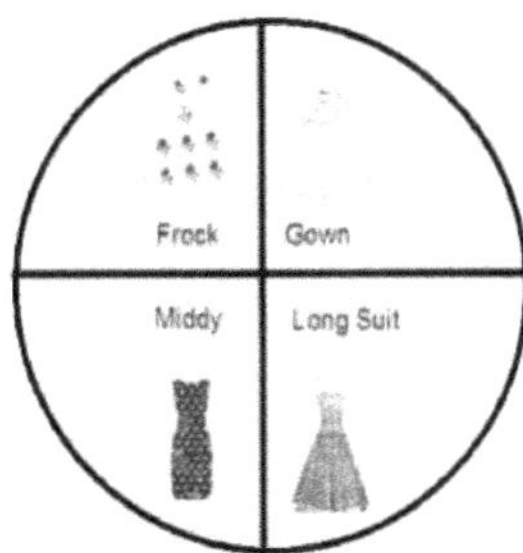

21. What will she wear after 3 hours?
    (a) Gown   (b) Middy

    (c) Frock   (d) Long Suit

22. What will she wear at 12 : 00 noon?

    (a) Long Suit

    (b) Frock

    (c) Middy

    (d) Gown

23. Which statement will makes this equation complete?

    54 _______ 62 _______ 23 _______ 78

    (a) >, >, >   (b) <, <, <

    (c) <, >, <   (d) <, <, >

24. The figure is made up of _________ triangles and _______ circles.

(a)   4 and 4   (b) 4 and 5

(c)   6 and 4   (d) 4 and 7

25. Arrange the sequence by using their numbers

(a)   1, 4, 2, 3, 5

(b)   1, 4, 2, 5, 3

(c)   2, 1, 3, 5, 4

(d)   3, 1, 2, 5, 4

Space for Rough Work

CYBER MOCK TEST 1-5

Name : __________

Number of Questions : 25

Max. Marks : 25

Time : 1 Hour

There is no negative marking in the test.

1. Which of the following is/are smart computer-based machine?

   (a) Mobile only
   (b) Palmtop only
   (c) Tablet only
   (d) All of these

2. Question given below is followed by four options. Choose the most appropriate option about computer.

   i. It is a man-made machine.
   ii. It needs electricity to work.
   iii. It works very fast and saves our time.
   iv. It can do many tasks simultaneously.

   (a) Only (i)
   (d) (ii) and (iii)
   (c) (i) and (iv)
   (d) All of these

3. In a computer, arithmetic logic unit (ALU) is a part of the

   (a) CPU   (b) CU
   (c) VDU   (d) MDU

Space for Rough Work

4. Modern computers are very reliable but they have no

    (a) common sense

    (b) learning power

    (c) feeling

    (d) all of these

5. One computer that is not considered a portable computer is

    (a) minicomputer

    (b) a laptop computer

    (c) tablet PC

    (d) all of these

6. Personal computers use a number of chips mounted on a main circuit board. What is the common name for such boards?

    (a) Billboard

    (b) Motherboard

    (c) Whiteboard

    (d) Breadboard

7. ____________ is any part of the computer that you can physically touch.

    (a) Hardware

    (b) Software

    (c) Windows operating system.

    (d) Application program.

8. Identify the given pictures.

    i.

    ii.

    (a) (i) RAM and (ii) UPS

    (b) (i) UPS and (ii) Power supply unit.

    (c) (i) Power supply unit and (ii) CPU

    (d) (i) Heater and (ii) Fan

9. A blinking symbol on the screen that shows where the next character will appear is

   (a) Delete key

   (b) Arrow key

   (c) Cursor

   (d) Return key

10. Identify input devices in the given picture.

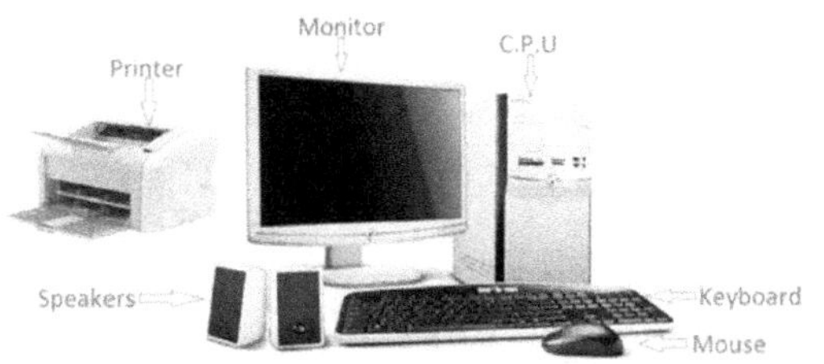

   (a) Mouse and Keyboard

   (b) Mouse, Printer and speaker

   (c) Keyboard, Monitor and CPU

   (d) None of these

11. What type of computer should be used to keep students records?

   (a) Mainframe computers

   (b) Supercomputers

   (c) Personal computers

   (d) All of these

12. A light-weight and compact machine, capable of doing everything which a desktop computer can do, is ____________.

   (a) 

   (b) 

   (c) 

   (d) 

Space for Rough Work

13. In railways, computers are mainly used for

    (a) issuing train tickets.

    (b) online reservation of train tickets.

    (c) preparing discharge slips of patients.

    (d) both a & b.

14. This is the key which is used to give space after words, alphabets or numbers. If pressed once, it gives the space of one character. It is _______.

    (a) 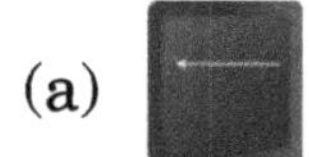

    (b) 

    (c) 

    (d) 

15. Which of the following keys should be pressed with symbol keys (present at the upper part of the keyboard) in order to type symbols?

    (a) 

    (b) 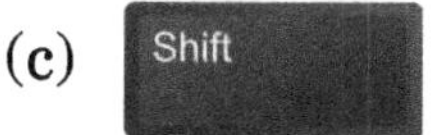

    (c) 

    (d) Alt

16. The name of some devices is given in jumbled form.

    (i) ISJTOCYK (ii) YEBKAODR (iii) OMUES

    Which of the following statements is CORRECT about all three of them?

    (a) (i) is used to enter data into computer while (ii) and (iii) are used to get data from the computer.

(b) Both (i) and (ii) are used to enter data into computer while (iii) is used to get data from the computer.

(c) Both (i) and (iii) are used to enter data into the computer while (ii) is used to get data from the computer.

(d) All three of them are used to enter data into the computer

17. Click the _______ mouse button twice quickly to _______ the icon, files or folders.

(a) right, copy

(b) left, open

(c) left, select

(d) right, select

18. With the help of a mouse, we can _______.

(a) point on file and folder

(b) draw and paint

(c) select multiple items

(d) all of these

19. Match the following mouse actions with their corresponding functions. Choose the correct option.

(i) Right-click	1. To move an object on the screen
(ii) Drag and drop	2. To display a list of commands
(iii) Click	3. To open a file or folders.
(iv) Double-click	4. To select a file or folders.

(a) i-3, ii-1, iii-4, iv-2

(b) i-2, ii-1, iii-4, iv-3

(c) i-4, ii-3, iii-2, iv-1

(d) i-1, ii-2, iii-4, iv-3

20. In the MS-Paint toolbox, the $\wedge\!\!\!/$ shape tool is used to draw ________.

    (a) open curves

    (b) straight lines only

    (c) stars only

    (d) all of these

21. MS-Paint can be used to ________.

    (a) draw pictures

    (b) open images

    (c) color pictures

    (d) all of these

22. Which of the following types of tools is used to draw the different kinds of brushes in MS-Paint?

    (a)   (b)

    (c)   (d)

23. Which of the following statements is/are correct about an App?

    (a) It is application software.

    (b) It is designed to help the user to perform specific tasks.

    (c) It is available freely or at a nominal price.

    (d) All of these

24. Which of the following is the latest windows operating system?

    (a) Windows vista
    (b) Windows 8
    (c) Windows 10
    (d) Windows 11

25. Which of the following is the correct sequence of Windows operating system in order of their released date? Choose the correct option.

(a) Windows XP, windows vista, windows 7, windows 8, windows 10

(b) Windows vista, windows 7, Windows 8, windows XP, windows 10

(c) Windows 7, windows 8, windows 10, windows XP, windows vista

(d) Windows vista, windows XP, windows 7, windows 8, windows 10

OLYMPIAD
Mock Test

Name : _______

Max. Marks : 25

Number of Questions : 25

Time : 1 Hour

There is no negative marking in the test.

1. Select the hand-held pocket device, which can be connected with the desktop computer using a wire or data cable.

(a)   (b)

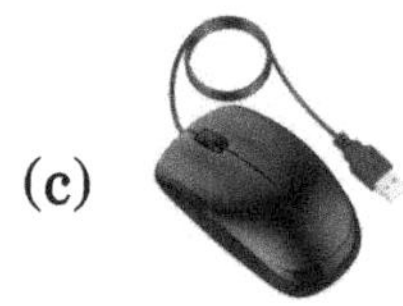

(c)   (d)

2. Which of the following types of smart computers are capable of supporting many hundreds or thousands of users simultaneously?

(a) Palmtop

(b) Mainframe computer

(c) Laptop

(d) Super computer

3. Which of the following types of smart computers performs hundreds of millions of instructions per second?

(a) Palmtop

(b) Mainframe computer

(c) Laptop

(d) Super computer

4. Match the column-1 and column-2 given in the following table. Choose the correct option.

	Column-1		Column-2
(i)	Windows	1	It is a background picture on the screen.
(ii)	Screensaver	2	Screen that appears once the computer is switch on.
(iii)	Desktop	3	It is an operating system that runs your computer
(iv)	Wallpaper	4	It is a computer program that blanks the screen or fills it with moving images or patterns when the computer is not in use for a particular time period.

(a) i-3,ii-4,iii-2,iv-1

(b) i-2,ii-1,iii-4,iv-3

(c) i-4,ii-3,iii-2,iv-1

(d) i-1,ii-4,iii-2,iv-3

5. On the desktop screen, several small pictures are seen. These pictures are called

(a) scions

(b) icons

(c) pictures

(d) tinos

6. How can you take proper care of your computer?

(a) By keeping it in a cool and dust-free room.

(b) By allowing dust and moisture around the computer.

(c) By keeping it in a hot room.

(d) By keeping it in an open ground.

7. Which of the following is not an output device?

    (a) Monitor   (b) Printer

    (c) Keyboard   (d) Speakers

8. Identify the given devices.

    i.   ii.

    (a) (i) RAM and (ii) NIC Card

    (b) (i)ROM and (ii) Mother board

    (c) (i)Floppy disk and (ii) RAM

    (d) (i)Hard disk and (iii) ROM

9. The devices on a computer system that let you see the processed information is known as ___________ device.

    (a) input

    (b) output

    (c) storage

    (d) none of these

10. In office, computers are used to _______.

    (a) type letters

    (b) prepare presentations

    (c) search information

    (d) all of these.

11. Computer helps scientists mainly in

    (a) launching rockets and satellites.

    (b) maintaining the direction of rockets and satellites.

    (c) making building layouts

    (d) both (a) and (b)

12. Computer in banks can be used to maintain

    (a) records of customers

    (b) processing transaction

    (c) cash records

    (d) all of these

———————— Space for Rough Work ————————

13. This is the key which is used to remove the words. If pressed once, it gives the backspace of one character. It is _______.

(a) 

(b) 

(c) 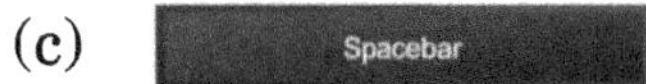

(d) Shift

14. What is the use of the Windows key on the keyboard?

(a) It is opens a new window.

(b) It closes the current application.

(c) It opens the start menu.

(d) It closes the all the open window.

15. Which of the following statements is incorrect?

(a) Caps-lock key is used to insert capital letters.

(b) Enter key is the longest key on the keyboard

(c) There are two Alt, Ctrl, and Shift keys on the keyboard.

(d) There are 12 function keys on the keyboard.

16. When more than one item has been selected, it can be done with the help of the mouse by

(a) double clicking and selecting the more than one item.

(b) dropping all the items.

(c) clicking and dragging.

(d) triple clicking.

17. Which of the following mouse actions is correct, if you want icon to be highlighted on the screen?

   (a) Right-click on this icon

   (b) Left double click on this icon

   (c) Left click on this icon

   (d) Right double click on this icon

18. The tool used to spray colours on the image is

   (a) 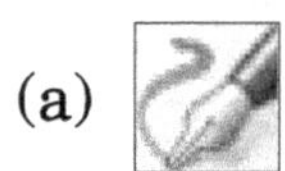   (b) 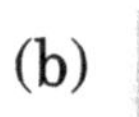 

   (c) 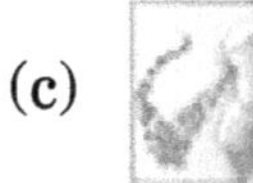   (d)  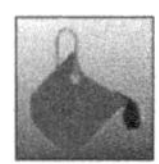

19. The tool used to select the rectangular portion of an image is __________.

   (a) 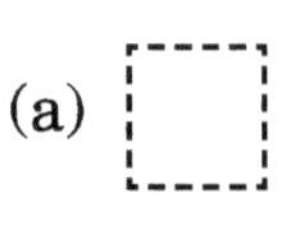   (b) 

   (c)    (d) 

20. Match the column-1 and column-2 given below. Choose the correct option.

   (i) Polygon   1. 

   (ii) Oval   2. 

   (iii) Rectangle   3.

   (iv) Rounded rectangular symbol   4. 

   (a) i-4,ii-3,iii-1,iv-2
   (b) i-2,ii-4,iii-1,iv-3
   (c) i-4,ii-3,iii-2,iv-1
   (d) i-1,ii-2,iii-4,iv-3

21. For the proper working of a computer, a mouse should always kept on a

   (a) rugged/rough table surface
   (b) mouse pad made of glass
   (c) mouse pad made of rubber or foam
   (d) mouse pad made of plastic

22. iPad, Google Nexus and Microsoft Surface are examples of _______ computers.

    (a) desktop computer

    (b) super computer

    (c) laptop

    (d) tablet

23. The given device can be read by

    (a) Smart phones

    (b) Action camera

    (c) Tablets

    (d) All of these

24. Which of the following is/are gaming devices?

    (a) Play station

    (b) Game boy

    (c) Game cube

    (d) All of these

25. Which of the following famous games is shown below?

    (a) Hill Climb Racing

    (b) Need for Speed

    (c) Angry Birds

    (d) Candy Crush Saga

Name : __________   Max. Marks : 25

Number of Questions : 25   Time : 1 Hour

There is no negative marking in the test.

1. Which of the following jumbled words can complete the sentence given below?

    Computer is a ________ machine.

    (a) DIGIR   (b) BUDM

    (c) LOWS   (d) MARTS

2. Identify the following.

    I. It is used to search street locations, thus helps the travelers from getting lost.

    II. It works when internet connection is available.

    III. It is known as GPS.

(a)

(b)

(c)

(d) Both (a) and (b)

———— Space for Rough Work ————

3. Select the correct match.

	Column-1		Column-2
(i)		1.	It is a portable and compact personal computer with the same capabilities as a desktop computer.
(ii)		2.	It is a device which makes a persistent human readable representation of graphics or text on paper.
(iii)		3.	It is a wireless, portable personal computer with a touchscreen interface. It is smaller than a notebook computer, but larger than a smart phone.
(iv)		4.	It is not portable, which means you cannot carry it wherever you want to.

    (a) i-4, ii-3,iii-1,iv-2   (b) i-2, ii-1,iii-4,iv-3

    (c) i-4, ii-3,iii-2,iv-1   (d) i-1, ii-4,iii-2,iv-3

————————————————— Space for Rough Work —————————————————

4. BIOS stand for

    (i) Basic Input-Output System

    (ii) Basic Interrupted-Output System

    (a) Only (ii)

    (b) Only (i)

    (c) Both (i) and (ii)

    (d) None of these

5. A computer gathers data, processes it, outputs the data or information, and ___________ the data or information.

    (a) retrieve   (b) delete

    (c) stores   (d) move

6. Hard disk drives and CD drives are examples of ___________ devices.

    (a) input device

    (b) output device

    (c) storage device

    (d) none of these

7. What difference does the 5th generation computer have from other generation computers?

    (a) Technological advancement

    (b) Scientific code

    (c) Object Oriented Programming

    (d) All of the above

8. Which of the following statements is/are correct about the jumbled word?

NRMOITO

I. It shows whatever you type on the keyboard or draw with the mouse.

II. It looks like a TV screen.

    (a) Only 2

    (b) Both 1 and 2

    (c) Neither 1 and 2

    (d) Only 1

9. Identify the given devices.

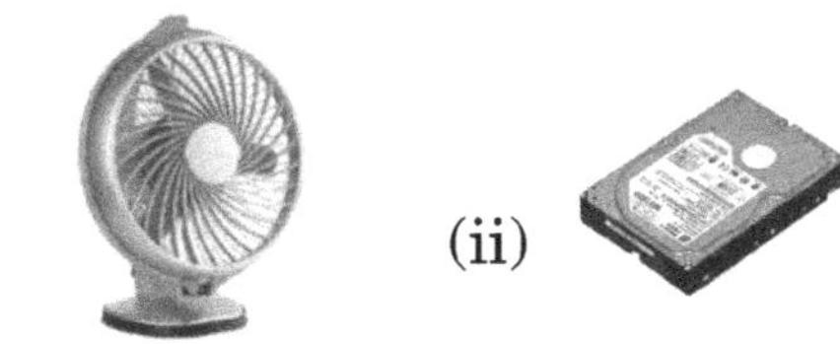

(i)   (ii)

(a) (i) Motherboard and (ii) RAM

(b) (i) Fan and (ii) RAM

(c) (i) Heat Sink Processor Fan and (ii) Hard disk

(d) (i) CPU and (ii) Floppy disk

10. Which of the following statements holds true regarding the use of computer in hospitals?

I. Computer in hospitals is used for withdrawal of money at the ATM.

II. Computer in hospitals is also used for controlling machines in sick room for performing operations and surgeries.

III. Computer in hospitals is used to maintain case histories of patient's records and also preparing discharge slips.

(a) Only 2

(b) Both 1 and 2

(c) Both 2 and 3

(d) Both 1 and 3

11. In India, computer is used in many fields, but there are few areas where computer is rarely used. In a which field computer is less used?

(a) Banks   (b) Defense

(c) Medicine   (d) Farming

12. Match the column-1 and column-2 given in the following table. Choose the correct option.

	Column-1		Column-2
(i)	Computer for entertainment	1.	For communication
(ii)	Computer in defense	2.	For surgery
(iii)	Computer in hospitals	3.	For teaching
(iv)	Computer in schools	4.	For playing games

   (a) i-4,ii-1,iii-2,iv-3   (b) i-2,ii-1,iii-4,iv-3
   (c) i-4,ii-3,iii-2,iv-1   (d) i-1,ii-4,iii-2,iv-3

13. Which key combination will be use to insert the '@' symbol in a document?

   (a)  Shift + @ 2

   (b) Ctrl + @ 2

   (c) Alt + @ 2

   (d)  Caps Lock + @ 2

14. When Numlock Num Lock key is off on the keyboard, pressing 1 End key on numeric pad

   (a) will perform page down operation.

   (b) will insert 1 in the document.

   (c) will perform page up operation.

   (d) will move the cursor to the end of the line.

———————————— Space for Rough Work ————————————

15. Match the column-1 and column-2 given in the following table. Choose the correct option.

	Column-1		Column-2
(i)	Key used to go to the next line	1.	Spacebar
(ii)	Key used to type in capital letters	2.	Enter
(iii)	Key used to insert spaces	3.	Backspace
(iv)	Key used to remove text to the left of the cursor	4.	Caps Lock

(a) i-2,ii-4,iii-1,iv-3   (b) i-2,ii-1,iii-4,iv-3

(c) i-4,ii-3,iii-2,iv-1   (d) i-1,ii-4,iii-2,iv-3

16. Which of the following statements holds true regarding double click?

I. To release the left mouse button after pressing it twice quickly is called double click.

II. Double click is used to open an item.

(a) Only 1
(b) Both 1 and 2
(c) Only 2
(d) Neither 1 Nor 2

Space for Rough Work

17. Which of the following mouse operations when used in combination with Ctrl key selects multiple items on the screen?

    (a) Right click and drag
    (b) Multiple left click
    (c) Double Right click and drop
    (d) Double Left click and drop

18. Match the column-1 and column-2 given in the following table. Choose the correct option.

(i) Joystick	1. 
(ii) Optical mouse	2. 
(iii) Stylus	3. 
(iv) Trackball	4.

(a) i-3,ii-1,iii-4,iv-2

(b) i-2,ii-1,iii-4,iv-3

(c) i-4,ii-3,iii-2,iv-1

(d) i-1,ii-2,iii-4,iv-3

19. The tool used for desired shape selection of the image is __________

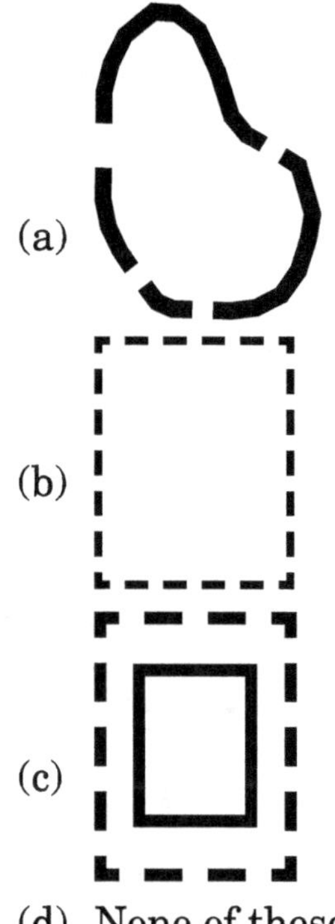

(a)

(b)

(c)

(d) None of these

20. Select the INCORRECT match

    (a) To select any irregularly desired shaped part of an image - 

    (b) To select any rectangular or square portion of an image 

    (c) To select the whole portion of an image - 

    (d) To delete the selected object- 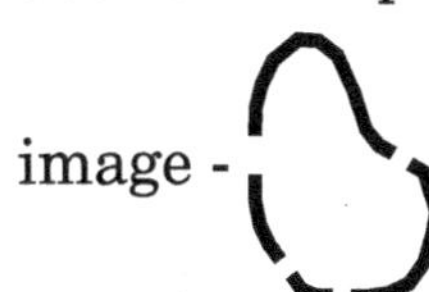

21. Files created in paint are by default saved as............files.

    (a) .JPEG   (b) .PNG

    (c) .GIF   (d) .TIFF

22. What is the latest version of the famous game 'Candy Crush Saga'?

    (a) Candy Crush Apple Saga

    (b) Candy Crush Mango Saga

    (c) Candy Crush Jelly Saga

    (d) Candy Crush Orange Saga

23. Kitkat, lollipop, jelly bean, icecream sandwich are the versions of __________.

    (a) Microsoft operating system

    (b) Windows operating system

    (c) Android operating system

    (d) Apple operating system

24. iPhone is a line of smart phones designed by a............

    (a) Google Inc.

    (b) Apple Inc.

    (c) Samsung Inc.

    (d) Intex Inc.

25. What is/iPod Nano?

    (a) Apple's fastest mobile phone

    (b) Apple's latest tablet PC

    (c) A version of the popular itunes.

    (d) A small portable media player produced by Apple Inc.

HINTS & EXPLANATIONS

ENGLISH

MOCK TEST 1

ANSWER KEY									
1	(d)	**9**	(a)	**17**	(d)	**25**	(d)	**33**	(c)
2	(b)	**10**	(b)	**18**	(b)	**26**	(a)	**34**	(a)
3	(d)	**11**	(c)	**19**	(b)	**27**	(b)	**35**	(a)
4	(d)	**12**	(b)	**20**	(b)	**28**	(b)	**36**	(a)
5	(c)	**13**	(c)	**21**	(b)	**29**	(a)	**37**	(b)
6	(b)	**14**	(a)	**22**	(a)	**30**	(b)	**38**	(a)
7	(a)	**15**	(b)	**23**	(a)	**31**	(a)	**39**	(b)
8	(b)	**16**	(a)	**24**	(c)	**32**	(b)	**40**	(a)

1. (d) Student

2. (b) Letter

3. (d) Frog

4. (d) Bread: Cheese

5. (c) Wealthy

6. (b) Another

7. (a) Breathe

8. (b) The wolves are related to dogs and foxes.

9. (a) He is happy playing with his friends but sad when he's studying.

10. (b) Carry your woollens to Shimla as it would be cold there.

11. (c) I come between Friday and Sunday. I am Saturday.

12. (b) The hare ran faster than the tortoise.

13. (c) This is my ball. I will not give it to you.

14. (a) I saw the sunset.

15. (b) The birds make their nest in trees.

16. (a) There is a girl sitting on that bench.

17. (d) I go to school at 7:30 every day.

18. (b) The girl is playing in the sand.

19. (b) The dog is hiding behind the door.

20. (b) You cannot enter because you are late.

21. (b) Sheena has to break the rules, if she has to enter the palace.

22. (a) Mrs. Paula was fond of gardening.

23. (a) One day she noticed that her plants were infected.

24. (c) She disagreed on using pesticides because they would make the plants poisonous.

25. (d) Synonym of vast is huge.

26. (a) This letter is written to a friend.

27. (b) Sam is very good in studies.

28. (b) Danny is suggesting Sam to do exercise.

29. (a) We must pay as much attention to studies as to physical activities.

30. (b) Meena: Have you read this book?

Sheena: No, I haven't.

31. (a) Rahul: I forgot to bring my pens. Can you please give me one pen?

Nazia: Yes, sure.

32. (b) Hello, my name is Dev. What's your name?

Akshat: I am Akshat.

33. (c) Cindy: Can you please tell me the answer of this question?

Laura: Yes, sure.

34. (a) Krish: I went to the zoo yesterday.

Shyam: Great! What did you see there?

35. (a) Aryan: Is this your bag?

Kashish: Yes, it's mine.

36. (a) He is going to his office.
He will reach his office at 9:30 a.m.

37. (b) Bankeylal is a postman.
He delivers letters.

38. (a) Waiter: Good afternoon! What can I get for you?
Some starters, please!

39. (b) We should plant trees to protect our earth otherwise our earth will be destroyed.

40. (a) We should always check the expiry of the things we buy.
We might use expired things and fall sick.

MOCK TEST 2

ANSWER KEY									
1	(a)	8	(b)	15	(b)	22	(b)	29	(b)
2	(d)	9	(b)	16	(d)	23	(b)	30	(b)
3	(b)	10	(a)	17	(a)	24	(b)	31	(b)
4	(d)	11	(b)	18	(a)	25	(d)	32	(a)
5	(a)	12	(d)	19	(d)	26	(c)	33	(b)
6	(a)	13	(d)	20	(c)	27	(b)	34	(a)
7	(b)	14	(b)	21	(b)	28	(c)	35	(c)

1. **(a)** Cucumber. Rest are all fruits. Cucumber is not.
2. **(c)** Circle. Circle has no lines.
3. **(b)** Knife
4. **(d)** Sing. Rest are all animal sounds, sing is not.
5. **(a)** Go and play football.
6. **(a)** I am mostly black in colour, I grow on your head. I am hair.
7. **(b)** You wear me when you feel cold.

   I am a sweater.
8. **(b)** You promised me that you will study.
9. **(b)** He has borrowed that book from the library.
10. **(a)** I went to school with my friend.
11. **(b)** Can you go there?
12. **(d)** Shally brought a bouquet of flowers.
13. **(d)** The lion roared to scare the other animals.
14. **(b)** We must never waste food.
15. **(b)** A place near the sea is called a beach.
16. **(d)** They're all going to watch the movie.
17. **(a)** We used waste to make the puppets.
18. **(a)** When I met him, he seemed to have grown taller.
19. **(d)** Zoologist studies animals.
20. **(c)** You will have to put in more effort.
21. **(b)** Water, air and food
22. **(b)** The kings also need air, water and food.
23. **(b)** When we want to write, we all use pen.
24. **(b)** We read a book.
25. **(d)** There was a bomb in the plane.
26. **(c)** The police activity
27. **(b)** It detects bombs and diffuses them.
28. **(c)** When the passengers came to know the reason of landing, they were scared.
29. **(b)** After about three hours, we were able to fly.
30. **(b)** Sheena: Hello, Ayan, where had you been?

    Ayan : I had gone to Austria.
31. **(b)** Fred: How's America?

    Harris: It's a lovely place.
32. **(a)** Student: When can I meet the Principal?

    Peon: He is free tomorrow after 12:30.
33. **(b)** Ram: Would you like to come for dinner tomorrow?

    Rohit: Sorry, it's my sister's birthday tomorrow.
34. **(a)** John: I was late for work , I got up very late.

    Steve: Try to get up early.
35. **(c)** Customer: How much for this watch?

    Shopkeeper: Rs. 1000. It shows date and month also.

MOCK TEST 3

ANSWER KEY

1	(d)	9	(b)	17	(c)	25	(c)	33	(c)
2	(d)	10	(b)	18	(b)	26	(a)	34	(b)
3	(b)	11	(a)	19	(a)	27	(b)	35	(d)
4	(d)	12	(a)	20	(b)	28	(b)	36	(c)
5	(b)	13	(a)	21	(b)	29	(a)	37	(b)
6	(c)	14	(b)	22	(c)	30	(b)	38	(d)
7	(b)	15	(a)	23	(c)	31	(a)	39	(a)
8	(a)	16	(a)	24	(b)	32	(b)	40	(c)

1. **(d)** Horse

2. **(d)** Musician

3. **(b)** Peacock

4. **(d)** Meal

5. **(b)** Nose

6. **(c)** Begin

7. **(b)** School

8. **(a)** Mr. Ben is a doctor. He is a child specialist.

9. **(b)** I have bought an aquarium for my house.

10. **(b)** I live on the seventh floor of the building.

11. **(a)** I love my country India. I have lived here since birth.

12. **(a)** Do you have a spare shirt?

13. **(a)** The postman delivers letters in this area.

14. **(b)** How much did you pay for this dress?

15. **(a)** I wanted to drink some cold drink not hot tea.

16. **(a)** Elephant : trumpets :: Horse : neighs

17. **(c)** Food to grow : Exercise to stay fit

18. **(b)** Earth is a planet: Moon is a satellite

19. **(a)** Seawater is salty.

20. **(b)** I want to eat a piece of cake.

21. **(b)** This poem talks of a butterfly.

22. **(c)** The butterfly has colourful wings.

23. **(c)** It sits on flowers.

24. **(b)** We can't catch it because it will fly away.

25. **(c)** According to me wings of a butterfly are soft.

26. **(a)** Ken was scared of swimming.

27. **(b)** His sister used to make fun of him.

28. **(b)** Ken was scared of going to pool because he thought he will drown.

29. (a) On the day they went to pool, they realised that they had so much to share.

30. (b) Tom : Can you tell me the time?
Tim: It's quarter past nine.

31. (a) Yan: What are they doing?
Yang: I don't know. Let's go and see.

32. (b) Pam : Have you seen my book? I can't find it.
Laura: Did you look for it in your cupboard?

33. (c) Asha: When will the movie start?
Abha: At 5:50.

34. (b) Thanks for saving my life.

35. (d) Vedant: Do you have a hobby?
Ved: Yes, I love collecting stamps.

36. (c) Can you add a spoon of sugar to the tea?

37. (b) He cannot write because he has hurt his thumb.

38. (d) Sheep

39. (a) One baby, many babies

40. (c) Poly: I want to learn guitar. What about you?
Paul: I also want to.

MOCK TEST 4

ANSWER KEY									
1	(a)	8	(a)	15	(b)	22	(b)	29	(b)
2	(d)	9	(b)	16	(b)	23	(b)	30	(b)
3	(d)	10	(b)	17	(b)	24	(a)	31	(a)
4	(d)	11	(b)	18	(a)	25	(b)	32	(b)
5	(b)	12	(b)	19	(b)	26	(b)	33	(c)
6	(b)	13	(b)	20	(c)	27	(b)	34	(a)
7	(b)	14	(b)	21	(c)	28	(a)	35	(c)

1. (a) Bread. All others are things we can drink, bread is to be eaten.

2. (d) Car. All others are two-wheeled vehicles, car is a four-wheeled vehicle.

3. (d) Horse. All others are water animals, horse is a land animal.

4. (d) Chess. All others are outdoor games, chess is an indoor game.

5. (b) Push

6. (b) Hospital

7. (b) Children

8. (a) Fifty comes before fifty one.

9. (b) Did you hear the howl of a fox?

10. (b) Are you reading this book?

11. (b) His mother makes tasty food.

12. (b) This cloth is very rough, give me smooth cloth.

13. (b) This is a Eucalyptus tree. It gives us many medicines.

14. (b) There is so much work to do.

15. (b) Go there, you will find a shop.

16. (b) Give me a scoop of ice cream

17. (b) Miss Rita is a writer. Her writings are liked by children.

18. (a) It is always said no news is good news.

19. (b) I was a very bright student in my school days. I always came first in class.

20. (c) Every morning I take my dog for a walk.

21. (c) The boy was cute.

22. (b) The boy wanted to be strong.

23. (b) He loved watching movies.

24. (a) His mother did not like his movie watching.

25. (b) Finally the boy went to the school.

26. (b) Dam was a dragon girl.

27. (b) Nothing

28. (a) To look for food

29. (b) Papaya

30. (b) Meena: This is my uncle Sam, he stays in Africa.
Sheena: Nice to meet you.

31. (a) Fanny: Please put on the lights, I cannot see anything.
Sam: Sure.

32. (b) Tom : Ms. Jane, is it your first trip to Mumbai?
Jane : Yes, everything is new to me. Mumbai is lovely.

33. (c) Nisha: What time will you go for shopping?
Rita: At 7:30.

34. (a) Dad: Sonu, why have you broken that glass?
Sonu : I am so sorry, it was by mistake.

35. (c) Doctor : I am giving you a few medicines, take them on time.
Patient: Sure, I'll take them.

MOCK TEST 5

ANSWER KEY									
1	(d)	8	(c)	15	(a)	22	(a)	29	(b)
2	(d)	9	(b)	16	(b)	23	(a)	30	(a)
3	(d)	10	(c)	17	(a)	24	(d)	31	(b)
4	(c)	11	(c)	18	(c)	25	(c)	32	(a)
5	(b)	12	(a)	19	(b)	26	(a)	33	(b)
6	(a)	13	(c)	20	(a)	27	(a)	34	(b)
7	(b)	14	(d)	21	(b)	28	(b)	35	(b)

1. **(c)** Glove

2. **(a)** Rice

3. **(d)** Desk, rest all are found in home.

4. **(c)** Fish

5. **(b)** Broom

6. **(a)** Neck

7. **(b)** Please

8. **(c)** Manish's parents had gone to school. They went by car.

9. **(b)** He saw an octopus in the river.

10. **(c)** One woman: Many women

11. **(c)** Goat bleats: Crow croaks

12. **(a)** If light is to summer than dark is to winter.

13. **(c)** The monkey is jumping on the tree.

14. **(d)** You go and make peace with him.

15. **(a)** My friend stays in Australia. She has two children.

16. **(b)** I have won the trophy. I ran very fast.

17. **(a)** He will not be able to attend the concert because he is not there in town.

18. **(c)** Earth revolves around the Sun.

19. **(b)** I want to gift you this doll. Now it is yours.

20. **(a)** Who is the principal's son? Have you met him?

21. **(b)** The king was fond of listening to praises.

22. **(a)** His son knew that all praises were false.

23. **(a)** The king asked his ministers about the most wise king in the world.

24. **(d)** One minister sat quietly because he was scared of speaking the truth.

25. **(c)** He had promised him safety of life.

26. **(a)** To the zoo

27. **(a)** He saw a monkey swinging here and there.

28. **(b)** He saw a bear; it was too big.

29. **(b)** The lion was in its den.

30. **(a)** Rohan: Did you live in tents?
Rohit: Yes, we did.

31. **(b)** Mr Glenn: Who cooks food for you?
Mr.James: I cook my own food.

32. **(a)** Amit: Why are trees so tall in Kerela?
Sumit: That's because Kerela gets a lot of rain.

33. **(b)** Sharon: Whose picture is this?
Shan: It is mine.

34. **(b)** Steve: Whose is that white car?
Deb: It belongs to my friend.

35. **(b)** Tim: Let's go to the museum today.
Sim: Sure, what time?

MATHEMATICS

MOCK TEST 1

ANSWER KEY

1	(a)	8	(d)	15	(a)	22	(b)	29	(b)
2	(c)	9	(a)	16	(c)	23	(a)	30	(a)
3	(c)	10	(d)	17	(a)	24	(b)	31	(c)
4	(c)	11	(c)	18	(c)	25	(b)	32	(c)
5	(b)	12	(b)	19	(c)	26	(c)	33	(a)
6	(c)	13	(b)	20	(b)	27	(d)	34	(c)
7	(d)	14	(a)	21	(a)	28	(c)	35	(d)

1. (a) 89 has 8 tens.

T	O
8	9

2. (c) The digit at the place of tens is 1.

H	T	O
8	1	2

3. (c)

$$
\begin{array}{l}
\text{H T O} \\
\text{2 3 9} \\
\quad 9 \times 1 = 9 \\
\quad 3 \times 10 = 30 \\
\quad 2 \times 100 = 200
\end{array}
$$

Hence, place value of 3 is 30.

4. (c) Glass can slide and roll.

5. (b) $26 + 38 + 19 + 14 = 97$

6. (c) $54 + 45 = 99$

7. (d) Total number of mangoes = 14

Total number of apples = 12

Total number of watermelon = 1

Total number of bananas = 6

$14 + 12 + 1 + 6 = 33$

Therefore, she bought 33 fruits.

8. (d) Total number of people = 128 + 25 = 153

9. (a) Total number of students in a school = 520

Number of students absent on Thursday = 38

Number of students present on Thursday = 520 – 38

$$= 482$$

10. (d) Number of eggs = 624

Number of rotten eggs = 15

Total number of eggs in good condition = 624 – 15 = 609

11. (c) Number of days in a week = 7

Total number of days in 4 weeks = 7× 4 = 28 days

12. (b) 6 should be multiplied with 9 to get 54

$9 \times \boxed{6} = 54$

13. (b) Total number of ice creams = 112

Total number of girls = 7

Each girl will get $112 \div 7 = 16$ ice creams

$$7 \overline{\smash{)}112}(16$$
$$\underline{-7}\downarrow$$
$$42$$
$$\underline{42}$$
$$0$$

14. (a) $2\overline{\smash{)}86}(43 \longrightarrow$ Quotient
$$\underline{-8}\downarrow$$
$$06$$
$$\underline{06}$$
$$0$$

15. (a) Total length of tape = 36 m

Tape used = 23 m

Tape left = 36 – 23 m = 13 m

16. (c) Any number subtracted by zero gives the number itself.

17. (a) Total bags of rice = 10

Weight of each bag = 5 kg

Total weight of 10 bags

= 10 × ×5 = 50 kg

18. (c) Hourhand is between 3 and 4. Minute hand is at 6. The time is 3:30.

19. (c) October comes after September

20. (b) (A)→3, (B)→4, (C)→1, (D)→2,

21. (a) There are 30 days in the month of september

22. (b) 28th September falls on Tuesday.

23. (a) Total number of parts = 3

Total number of shaded part = 1

Fraction of shaded part

$= \dfrac{\text{No. of shaded part}}{\text{Total number of part}} = \dfrac{1}{3}$

Therefore, fraction of shaded region $= \dfrac{1}{3}$

24. (b) Total number of parts = 9

Total number of unshaded parts = 4

Fraction of unshaded part $= \dfrac{4}{9}$

25. (b) Each bag has 40 ÷ 4 = 10 sweets

No. of non-red sweets in each bag = 10 – 3 = 7

No. of non-red sweets in 4 bags = 7 × 4 = 28

26. (c) The given figure has 9 squares

27. (d) Total amount spent

= ₹235 + ₹362 = ₹597

28. (c)

29. (b) The number are decreasing by subtracting 2

$$\overset{-2}{\frown}\ \overset{-2}{\frown}\ \overset{-2}{\frown}\ \overset{-2}{\frown}$$
$$32\quad 30\quad 28\quad 26\quad \underline{24}$$

30. (a)

31. (c) The height of tree A = 6 metres

The height of tree B = (6 + 3)

The height of tree B

= 9 metres

32. (c) Mangoes purchased by Aditi = 8 kg

Mangoes given to Sudhi = 4 kg

Mangoes left with Aditi

= 8 – 4 = 4 kg

33. (a)

34. (c) July has most number of birthdays.

8 girls and 6 boys = 14

35. (d) There are 66 students in class 2.

MOCK TEST 2

ANSWER KEY

1	(b)	8	(a)	15	(d)	22	(b)	29	(a)
2	(d)	9	(b)	16	(c)	23	(d)	30	(c)
3	(d)	10	(d)	17	(b)	24	(c)	31	(c)
4	(a)	11	(d)	18	(b)	25	(c)	32	(b)
5	(a)	12	(a)	19	(c)	26	(b)	33	(a)
6	(c)	13	(c)	20	(a)	27	(c)	34	(a)
7	(b)	14	(a)	21	(a)	28	(c)	35	(b)

1. (b) Total number of chocolates

= 60

Total number of children = 5 (Nikki, Raja, Rani, Sachin, Kiran)

Number of chocolates each child will get = $60 \div 5$

$$
\begin{array}{r}
5\,)\,\overline{60}\,(12 \\
\underline{-5\downarrow} \\
10 \\
\underline{-10} \\
0
\end{array}
$$

Therefore, each child will get 12 chocolates.

2. (d) The sum of numbers from 1 to 10 is

$1 + 2 + 3 + 4 + 5 + 6 + 7 + 8 + 9 + 10 = 55$

3. (d) Eight hundred ninety seven = 897.

4. (a) Total number of pen stands = 9

Number of pens in each pen stand = 7

Therefore, total number of pens in 9 penstands = 9×7

= 63 pens.

5. (a) Total number of pages of books read by Ritu = 24

Total number of days to read = 12

Number of pages read by Ritu in 1 day = $24 \div 12 = 2$

$$
\begin{array}{r}
12\,)\,\overline{24}\,(2 \\
\underline{-24} \\
0
\end{array}
$$

6. (c) The number 843 has 8 hundreds.

7. (b) Amount spent on dress = ₹560

Amount spent on hand bag = ₹175

Total amount spent = ₹(560 + 175) = ₹735

Amount given to shopkeeper by Nisha = ₹1000

Amount returned by shopkeeper = ₹1000 − ₹735 = ₹265

Therefore, shopkeeper will return ₹265 to Nisha.

8. (a) Distance travelled by A = 56 km

Distance travelled by B = 48 km.

Difference between the distance travelled by A and B = 56 – 48 = 8 km

Therefore, 'A' travelled 8 km more than 'B'.

9. (b) 50 – 25 = 25

10. (d) Cone is not a flat shape.

11. (d) Score of Rahul = 126

Score of Sourav = 98

Total score of Rahul and Sourav = (126 + 98) = 224

12. (a) Number of mangoes is 1 box = 64

Number of mangoes in 5 boxes = 64 × 5 = 320

Therefore, total number of mangoes in 5 boxes = 320

13. (c) Price of a notebook = ₹125

Amount given by Avleen to the shopkeeper = ₹200

Amount returned by the shopkeeper ₹200 – ₹125 = ₹75.

14. (a) Number of apple trees = 85

Number of banana trees = 152

Number of guava trees = 125

Total number of trees in the garden = (85 + 152 + 125) = 362

15. (d) 37 is an odd number.

16. (c) Number of days in a leap year = 366

Number of days, Ronnie went to school = 288

Number of days, Ronnie did not go to school = 366 – 288 = 78 days

17. (b)

$$\begin{array}{r} H\ T\ O \\ 100 \\ +\ 20 \\ +\ \ \ 3 \\ \hline 123 \\ \hline \end{array}$$

18. (b) Total number of cups = 4

1 cup can hold = 50 ml

4 cups can hold = 4 × 50 ml = 200 ml

Therefore, 1 jug can hold 200 ml of water.

19. (c) 299 comes before 300.

20. (a) (A) → 3, (B) → 4, (C) → 1, (D) → 2

21. (a) The place value of 9 in 974 is 900.

22. (b) The minute hand is at 3 that means 15 minutes and the hour hand is between 7 and 8. Therefore, time shown by the clock is 7 : 15.

23. (d) 796 → Seven hundred and ninety six.

24. (c) July and August both have 31 days.

25. (c) A number multiplied by 1 gives number itself.

26. (b) Two hundred and fifty nine is written as 259.

27. (c) Numbers in (a), (b) and (d) are increasing by 1 but in (c) numbers are increasing by 100.

28. (c)

29. (a) Total number of pieces of cakes = 9

Pieces of cake distributed to friends = 4

Fraction of cake distributed to friends = $\dfrac{4}{9}$

30. (c) Total number of parts = 7

Number of unshaded parts = 4

Fraction of unshaded part = 4/7.

31. (c)

32. (b) 40 − 5 = 35

33. (a) She purchased 5 packets of biscuits.

34. (a) She purchased total 11 products.

35. (b) Biscuit has been purchased in maximum quantity.

$$\boxed{\textbf{MOCK TEST 3}}$$

ANSWER KEY											
1	(c)	8	(b)	15	(b)	22	(b)	29	(a)	36	(b)
2	(b)	9	(a)	16	(d)	23	(d)	30	(d)	37	(c)
3	(a)	10	(b)	17	(a)	24	(b)	31	(c)	38	(c)
4	(c)	11	(a)	18	(a)	25	(d)	32	(c)	39	(d)
5	(b)	12	(d)	19	(c)	26	(d)	33	(d)	40	(c)
6	(a)	13	(c)	20	(b)	27	(c)	34	(c)		
7	(a)	14	(c)	21	(a)	28	(c)	35	(d)		

1. (c) 5 tens = 50

4 ones = 4

50 + 4 = 54

2. (b)

3. (a) Marks scored by Snita in her first test = 48

Marks scored by Snita in her second test = 42

Total marks scored by Snita = 48 + 42 = 90

4. (c) A → 3, B → 4, C → 2, D → 1

5. (b) Number of marbles with Ravi = 150

Number of marbles with Sudhi = 132 marbles

Number of more marbles Ravi has than Sudhi = 150 −132 = 18

Ravi has 18 marbles more than Sudhi.

6. (a)

7. (a) Number of parts of circle = 6

Total number of coloured parts

= 4 (2 green + 1 blue + 1 red)

Number of uncoloured parts = 2

Fraction of uncoloured parts

$$= 2/6$$

8. (b) Book is the most expensive item.

9. (a) Eraser can be purchased.

10. (b) Radha is having 10 chocolates.

Reena has (6 + 10)

= 16 chocolates

Beena has 16 – 4 = 12 chocolates

11. (a) On Wednesday, maximum number of burgers were sold.

12. (d) 6 burgurs were sold on Thursday.

13. (c) On Monday and Friday sale of burgers was same.

14. (c)

15. (b) $56 \div 8 = 7$

$$8\,\overline{)56}\,(7$$
$$\underline{-\,56}$$
$$0$$

16. (d) The time shown in the clock is 6 : 15.

17. (a) A square has 4 sides.

18. (a)

19. (c) The price of vegetables = ₹340

Amount given to the shopkeeper = ₹500

Amount returned by the shopkeeper = ₹500 – ₹340

$$= ₹160$$

20. (b) Ice-creams produced in 1 day = 113

Ice-creams produced in 7 days

[1 week = 7 days] = 7 × 113

$$= 791$$

21. (a) 430 > 4 21

22. (b) The day after tomorrow will be Thursday.

23. (d) Total number of chairs = 660

Total number of rows = 10

Number of chairs in each row = 660 ÷ 10 = 66

$$10\,\overline{)660}\,(66$$
$$\underline{-60}$$
$$60$$
$$\underline{-60}$$
$$0$$

Number of chairs in each row is 66.

24. (b) 8 people are there in the queue.

25. (d) Circle does not have any sides and angles.

26. (d) Cone is a 3–D shape.

27. (c) 454 is the greatest number.

28. (c) The expanded form of 798 is 700 + 90 + 8.

29. (a) The duration of his dance class is 1 hour.

30. (d) In number 43, 3 is at one's place.

T	O
4	3

31. (c)

32. (c) Total number of students in a class = 60

Number of girls = 25 + 10 = 35

Hence, number of boys in the class = 60 − 35 = 25

33. (d) 16 glasses are required to fill the jug.

34. (c) 1 hour = 60 minutes

35. (d) 95 > 74 > 59 > 47

36. (b) Ice creams produced in one day = 20

Number of days in a week = 7

Since, Saturday is a holiday, so number of working days in a week = 6.

Ice creams produced in 6 days = 20 × 6 = 120.

Hence, 120 ice creams are produced in a week.

37. (c) $105 \div 5$

$$5\overline{)105}\,(21$$
$$\underline{-10}$$
$$\quad 05$$
$$\quad \underline{05}$$
$$\quad\quad 0$$

38. (c)

39. (d)
$$\begin{array}{r} 85 \\ \times\ 8 \\ \hline 680 \end{array}$$

680 can be written in expanded form as 600 + 80

40. (c) Weight of 1 sugar bag = 23 kg

Weight of 1 rice bag = 25 kg.

Total weight = 23 kg + 25 kg

= 48kg

MOCK TEST 4

ANSWER KEY

1	(d)	8	(c)	15	(c)	22	(a)	29	(c)
2	(d)	9	(a)	16	(c)	23	(b)	30	(b)
3	(c)	10	(d)	17	(b)	24	(b)	31	(b)
4	(d)	11	(a)	18	(d)	25	(c)	32	(a)
5	(b)	12	(c)	19	(b)	26	(c)	33	(c)
6	(b)	13	(b)	20	(b)	27	(a)	34	(a)
7	(c)	14	(d)	21	(a)	28	(a)	35	(c)

1. (d) 13 should be added to 13 to get 26.

2. (d)

T	O
8	5

There are 8 tens and 5 ones in 85.

3. (c) There are 3 sides in a triangle.

4. (d) The hour hand is between 4 and 5 and the minute hand is at 6 which means 30 minutes. Therefore, the time is 4 hours 30 mintues, i.e., 4 : 30.

5. (b) Number of pages read by Arup in a week = 60.

Total number of days in a week except Saturday = 6

$60 \div 6 = 10$

$$6\overline{)60}(10$$

Arup reads 10 pages in one day.

6. (b) 1 hour = 60 minutes

5 hours = $60 \times 5 = 300$ minutes.

7. (c) 1 bag contains = 5 kg wheat

10 bags contain = $5 \times 10 = 50$ kg

Therefore, 10 bags contain 50 kg wheat.

8. (c) 1 week = 7 days

4 weeks = $7 + 7 + 7 + 7$ = $4 \times 7 = 28$ days.

9. (a) The place value of 6 in 672 is 600

HTO
672
→2
→70
→600

10. (d) Number of legs a spider has = 8

Number of legs 3 spiders have $(8 + 8 + 8) = 24$

11. (a) Total number of chocolates = 457

Total number of chocolates distributed = 305

Number of chocolates left = $457 - 305 = 152$

$$\begin{array}{r} 457 \\ -305 \\ \hline 152 \end{array}$$

Therefore, 152 chocolates are left with Nishi.

12. (c) 1 hundred + 2 tens + 3 ones

= $100 + 20 + 3$

= 123

13. (b) Number of English novel = 381

Number of Comics = 249

Number of Story books = 186

Total number of books in the book shop = $381 + 249 + 186$

= 816

14. (d) $18 - 6 = 12 > 14 - 3 = 11$

15. (c) Passing marks of the test = 33

Marks scored by John = $5 + 33$

= 38

16. (c) Weight of a man before jogging = 83 kg

Weight of a man after two months = $83 - 15 = 68$ kg.

17. (b) 3 tens = 30

Then, the number after reducing 3 tens from 90 = $90 - 30 = 60$

18. (d) Total number of parts in the figure = 6

Number of unshaded parts = 4

Therefore, fraction of unshaded part in the given figure

$$= \frac{4}{6}.$$

19. (b) The age of father is 45 years.

20. (b) Age of grandfather is 62 years

Age of father is 45 years

Difference between the age of grandfather and father

$= 62 - 45 = 17$ years

21. (a)

22. (a) $32 + 5 = 37$

23. (b) $19 - 2 = 17$

24. (b) $53 - 37 = 16$

25. (c) Figure 'c' is a cone.

26. (c) Distance covered by Pia

= 20 metres

Distance covered by Naina

= 30 metres

Distance covered by Misha

= 35 metres

The distance covered by all girls

$= 20 + 30 + 35 = 85$ metres.

27. (a) Total number of parts = 5

Total number of shaded parts = 2

Fraction of the shaded portion = 2/5.

28. (a) Cost of a bat = ₹535

Cost of a ball = ₹127

Total amount he spent

$= ₹(535 + 127) = ₹662$

29. (c)

30. (b) If today is Monday, then Saturday will be after 4 days from Monday

31. (b) $21 - 7 = 14$

$17 - 3 = 14$

Therefore, $21 \boxminus 7 = 17 - 3$

32. (a) Eraser costs the least, i.e., ₹5.

33. (c) A toy car costs the most i.e. ₹80.

34. (a) The cost of pencil is ₹10.

35. (c) Both are true.

MOCK TEST 5

ANSWER KEY

1	(c)	8	(d)	15	(c)	22	(c)	29	(a)	36	(b)
2	(c)	9	(b)	16	(c)	23	(c)	30	(a)	37	(b)
3	(a)	10	(b)	17	(c)	24	(a)	31	(c)	38	(b)
4	(b)	11	(b)	18	(a)	25	(a)	32	(d)	39	(c)
5	(b)	12	(a)	19	(a)	26	(c)	33	(d)	40	(c)
6	(c)	13	(b)	20	(a)	27	(d)	34	(a)		
7	(c)	14	(a)	21	(d)	28	(a)	35	(c)		

1. (c) 99 is the odd number.

2. (c) Number of bananas = 6

Number of apples = 2

Number of mangoes = 8

Number of pineapple = 1

Total number of fruits in the basket are (6 + 2 + 8 + 1) = 17

3. (a)

H T O
9 4 7

The place value of 4 in 947 is 40.

4. (b) 445 + 341 = 786

5. (b) 657 − 238 = 419

6. (c) Books sold on Wednesday = 50

Books sold on Thursday = 50 + 10 = 60

Total books sold on Wednesday and Thursday = 50 + 60 = 110.

Therefore, total 110 books were sold on both the days.

7. (c) 1 hour = 60 minutes

$8 \text{ hours} = 60 \times 8 = 480 \text{ minutes}$.

Bulbul studies 480 minutes in a day.

8. (d) Beads used to make 1 chain = 96

Beads used to make 3 chains = 96 × 3 = 288.

9. (b) Number of parts in the figure = 8

Number of shaded parts in the figure = 2

Fraction of shaded part = $\dfrac{2}{8}$

10. (b) Cost of 1 chocolate = ₹10

Cost of 6 chocolates

= ₹(10 + 10 + 10 + 10 + 10 + 10)

= ₹60

11. (b) ₹100 + ₹20 + ₹10 + ₹5 + ₹2 + ₹1 = ₹138

12. (a) The nearest hundred for 534 is 500.

13. (b) November has 5 Mondays

14. (a) Time of train arrival = 5:00 pm

Anil waited at the railway station = 1 hour

Anil reached railway station 1 hour before the train arrived which means Anil reached railway station at 4 : 00 pm.

15. (c) Price of the video game = ₹205

Amount of money Radhika has = ₹185

Radhika needs ₹205 – ₹185 = ₹20 more to buy the video game.

16. (c) Total amount spent = ₹568 + ₹225 = ₹793

Amount returned by the shopkeeper = ₹800 – ₹793 = ₹7

17. (c) Total number of books = 9

Number of pages in each book = 20

Total number of pages in 9 books = 9 × 20 = 180 pages

18. (a) Total number of parts in the diagram = 8

Number of shaded parts = 3

Fraction of shaded part = 3/8

19. (a) Money saved by Sruthi in one day = ₹2

Money saved by Sruthi in 10 days = 2 × 10 = ₹20

20. (a) In the given clock the hour hand is at 7 and minute hand is at 3. Therefore, the time is 7 : 15.

21. (d) 29 February comes after every 4 years which is a leap year.

22. (c) The duration between

7:00 pm and 8:00 pm is 1 hour.

23. (c) Weight of 10 apples = Weight of 2 melons

Weight of 30 apples = Weight of 2 + 2 + 2 = 6 melons

24. (a)

25. (a) Option 'a' has 5 corners. b, c and d has 4 corners.

26. (c) The numbers are increasing by 3 numbers.

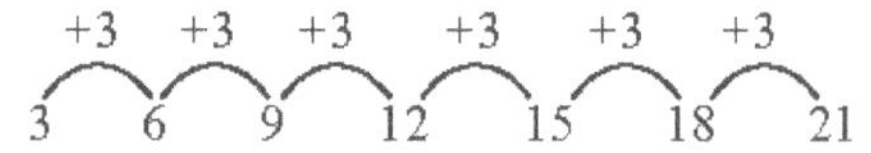

27. (d)

28. (a) There are 5 squares in the given figure.

29. (a) Distance travelled by car in 1 hour = 60 km

Distance travelled by car in 6 hours = 60 × 6 = 360 km

30. (a) Weight of a pencil is measured in grams.

31. (c) Total number of movie tickets = 24

Number of friends = 8

Movie   tickets   distributed

among friends $24 \div 8 = 3$

$$8\overline{)\,24\,}(3$$
$$\underline{-24}$$
$$0$$

Therefore, each friend got 3 movie ticket.

32. (d) $(A) \to 4, (B) \to 1, (C) \to 2, (D) \to 3$

33. (d) 15 children come to school by cycle.

34. (a) Least number of children come by car.

35. (c) Most of the children come by school bus.

36. (b) Number of children come by school bus = 17

Number of children come by car = 2

Then, number of more children come by bus than by car = $17 - 2 = 15$

Therefore, 15 more students come by school bus than by car.

37. (b) 300 ones = 3 hundreds

38. (b)

39. (c) $26 - 8 = 18$

Reena's birthday will come after 18 days.

40. (c) Bat is longest of pencil, ruler and hands pan.

SCIENCE

MOCK TEST 1

ANSWER KEY

1	(a)	6	(a)	11	(b)	16	(b)	21	(c)	26	(d)	31	(b)
2	(c)	7	(a)	12	(d)	17	(c)	22	(c)	27	(d)	32	(d)
3	(c)	8	(c)	13	(d)	18	(d)	23	(d)	28	(b)	33	(c)
4	(c)	9	(b)	14	(c)	19	(c)	24	(a)	29	(b)	34	(a)
5	(b)	10	(a)	15	(b)	20	(c)	25	(d)	30	(a)	35	(d)

1. **(a)** Tiger eats flesh.

2. **(c)** Cow can move from one place to another.

3. **(c)** Careless use of water.

4. **(c)** Hippopotamus is a wild animal.

5. **(b)** Oxygen is inhaled by human beings.

6. **(a)** Both living and non-living things are important for us.

7. **(a)** Pumpkin is a creeper.

8. **(c)** Scales

9. **(b)** Skin help to feel.

10. **(a)** My father's nephew or niece is my cousin.

11. **(b)** The person in the given figure is a cobbler.

12. **(d)** Leaves produces food.

13. **(d)** Sikhs go to Gurudwara to pray.

14. **(c)** Cotton yields fibre.

15. **(b)** Air fills space and has weight.

16. **(b)** Ear help us to hear the loud noise of aeroplane as well as the soft sound of bird.

17. **(c)** We can see the blue sky with our eyes.

18. **(d)** Chemist sells medicines.

19. **(c)** Sunflower shows movement.

20. **(c)** Bear is a wild animal which eats plant as well as animal.

21. **(c)** Rice is energy giving food, egg is a body building food, fruit is a protective food.

22. **(c)** The room shown in the given picture is kitchen.

23. **(d)**

24. **(a)** TAILOR.

25. **(d)** Do not run around the benches and climb on them and do not push or pull your friends while playing.

26. **(d)** Both band-aid and cotton should be kept in a first aid box.

27. **(d)** All these are the sources of mass communication.

28.(b) Republic Day is celebrated on 26 January every year.

29.(b) Kiran Bedi.

30.(a) Green vegetables gives fibre in the diet.

31.(b) Crow is an omnivorous animal.

32.(d) Cotton and jute are obtained from plants, silk is obtained from silk worm which is an animal.

33.(c) Skin senses hotness and coldness.

34.(a) Shreya is living in Kolkata.

35.(d) India Gate is located in New Delhi.

MOCK TEST 2

ANSWER KEY													
1	(a)	6	(b)	11	(d)	16	(a)	21	(a)	26	(a)	31	(c)
2	(a)	7	(b)	12	(b)	17	(b)	22	(d)	27	(b)	32	(c)
3	(d)	8	(b)	13	(b)	18	(c)	23	(a)	28	(b)	33	(d)
4	(d)	9	(a)	14	(d)	19	(b)	24	(c)	29	(d)	34	(c)
5	(d)	10	(a)	15	(b)	20	(b)	25	(b)	30	(d)	35	(d)

1. (a) Heart

2. (a) Snail

3. (d) We get oil from coconut, sunflower and mustard.

4. (d) In the absence of air, water and sunlight plants can not prepare their food.

5. (d) River is a natural non-living thing. Car and chair are non-living but man-made, Bird is a living thing.

6. (b)

7. (b) Stomach helps in digestion.

8. (b) A tent is a temporary house.

9. (a) Sachin Tendulkar is a famous personality in the field of cricket.

10.(a) Egg is a non-living thing. We can get a chicken from the egg which is a living organism.

11.(d)

12.(b) The given picture depicts that it's a winter season.

13.(b) Do not waste food.

14.(d) Fabric and tailor are needed to get school uniform stiched.

15.(b) Windows let in fresh air which is necessary for our lungs. Therefore a house without windows can makes us unwell.

16.(a) Imran will go to the Mosque to pray.

17.(b) We can send parcels and letters to different places through post office.

18.(c) If a house is dirty you need to clean it. A housekeeper helps in cleaning your house.

19.(b) Bladder stores urine before expelling it out.

20.(b) Carrom is a game which needs maximum four player to play.

21.(a) Rose is a flower.

22.(d) The animals shown in the picture are domestic animals and they are useful for human beings.

23.(a) Lion is a carnivorous animal therefore, it is an incorrect match.

24.(c) Group 1: Slowest means of transport; Group 2: Vehicles used for long distances.

25.(b) Biologist is the one who studies life.

26.(a) Gateway of India is situated in Mumbai. Howrah Bridge situated in kolkata, Marina Beach is situated in Chennai and Lal Quila is situated in Delhi.

27.(b) Lungs.

28.(b) Glass is a transparent as well as water proof material.

29.(d) Cotton and jute are natural fibres which we get from plants. Fruits also we get from plants.

30.(d) To keep the clothes germs free, wash them with good detergent and let them dry in the sun.

31.(c)

32.(c) Silkworm is used to produce silk.

33.(d) We eat leaves of spinach and coriander. Cabbage is a flower.

34.(c) Milk, oil and water are liquid in state. Cheese is solid in state.

35.(d) People of Mumbai speak marathi.

MOCK TEST 3

ANSWER KEY

1	(c)	6	(a)	11	(d)	16	(d)	21	(d)	26	(c)	31	(c)
2	(d)	7	(a)	12	(d)	17	(d)	22	(d)	27	(a)	32	(d)
3	(a)	8	(c)	13	(a)	18	(a)	23	(c)	28	(d)	33	(c)
4	(c)	9	(b)	14	(d)	19	(a)	24	(b)	29	(b)	34	(b)
5	(d)	10	(a)	15	(a)	20	(c)	25	(a)	30	(c)	35	(c)

1. **(c)** Sravan is using his sense of touch.

2. **(d)** Our muscles interact with bones to allow movement.

3. **(a)** Salt melts ice.

4. **(c)** Bicycle cannot be obtained from plants.

5. **(d)** All these statements are correct about the house.

6. **(a)** Cloud is a non-living thing.

7. **(a)** Wind Speed is measured by anemometer.

8. **(c)** Gas.

9. **(b)** Banana is seedless.

10. **(a)** Traffic Police.

11. **(d)** Cotton clothes should be worn while lighting crackers.

12. **(d)** Frog can grow.

13. **(a)** Egg is obtained from hen.

15. **(a)** Birds have wings.

16. **(d)** Evaporation is the process of changing water into water vapour.

17. **(d)** All these are protective foods.

18. **(a)** Water pollution causes death of marine animals.

19. **(a)** Meat of pig is called pork.

20. **(c)** Horse is used for transportation, dog is used four house keeping, sheep wool and we get mutton from goat.

21. **(d)** Walking on the footpath represents safety rule.

22. **(d)** Chameleon is known for changing colors.

23. **(c)** A life cycle is the series of changes that animal go through in life.

24. **(b)** Train.

25. **(a)** Sending and receiving of spoken or written message between people is called communication.

26. (c) Weather does not remain the same throughout the day it keeps changing.

27. (a) The animal shown in the picture is a dog. Dog is not a wild animal.

28. (d) Kidney, Lungs and Stomach are the internal part of body and ears are the external part of body.

29. (b) Air, glass jar and bubbles are transparent and book is opaque.

30. (c) These animals are omnivores.

31. (c) Donkey and camel are considered as 'Beast of Burden' which means working animals.

32. (d) Water and air both are very crucial for the survival of living beings.

33. (c) Plants which grow on the land is called terrestrial plant.

34. (b) Dance can be performed without water.

35. (c) Nylon, honey and plastic are not plant products.

MOCK TEST 4

ANSWER KEY

1.	(b)	6.	(c)	11.	(c)	16.	(a)	21.	(a)	26.	(c)	31.	(b)	36.	(a)
2.	(a)	7.	(d)	12.	(b)	17.	(c)	22.	(d)	27.	(d)	32.	(d)	37.	(b)
3.	(c)	8.	(b)	13.	(d)	18.	(b)	23.	(d)	28.	(c)	33.	(c)	38.	(d)
4.	(a)	9.	(c)	14.	(d)	19.	(c)	24.	(d)	29.	(c)	34.	(d)	39.	(b)
5.	(d)	10.	(c)	15.	(d)	20.	(a)	25.	(d)	30.	(a)	35.	(d)	40.	(c)

1. (b) 300 bones

2. (a) Eye $\Rightarrow$ See, Ear $\Rightarrow$ Hear, Nose $\Rightarrow$ Smell, Tongue $\Rightarrow$ Taste

3. (c) Wool protect us from cold.

4. (a) Windmill shows the direction of wind.

5. (d) Aeroplane is the means of transport.

6. (c) 4 (butter, milk, rice, sugar)

7. (d) Evaporation

8. (b) P O S T M A N

9. (c) Republic Day is celebrated on 26 January, Teacher's Day is celebrated on 5 September, Gandhi Jayanti is celebrated on 2 October and Children's Day is celebrated on 14 November.

10. (c) Train has more than 4 wheels.

11. (c) Boat and ship are water transport.

12. (b) Neem is a tree. Tulsi, mint and coriander are herbs.

13. (d) Cat, dog and rabbit are pet animal, Giraffe is a wild animal.

14. (d) Cotton, jute and silk are fibres. Socks is a fabric.

15. (d) Television, radio and newspaper are mass media. Telephone is a mode of communication.

16. (a) Summer, winter and monsoon are seasons.

17. (c) Victoria memorial is situated in Kolkata.

18. (b) Bungalow is a permanent house.

19. (c) Statement A and C are false. Moon changes its shape and stars are countless.

20. (a) The afternoon is usually the warmest.

21. (a) The smoke coming from the fire is a mixture of gases.

22. (d) A rainbow is visible in monsoon season only.

23. (d) Scavengers eats flesh from dead body of the living Organism.

24. (d) A house protects us from all (heat, cold, rain)

25. (d) Ravi is a carpenter. He makes door and repairs furniture.

26. (c) Fire station.

27. (d) All these statements are true.

28. (c) Exercise keeps bones and muscles strong.

29. (c) Putting your hand or head out of the window is a bad habit.

30. (a) Tiger lives in a jungle.

31. (b) Air is needed for burning.

32. (d) Carrot and radish are the examples of root.

33. (c) Spoon is made up of metal.

34. (d) A mechanic repairs vehicles.

35. (d) Albert Einstein worked in the field of science.

36. (a) Book has definite shape.

37. (b) Raincoat is used in monsoon season.

38. (d) Policeman and lawyer wear uniform.

39. (b) Water Cycle.

40. (c) Steam gets converted into water vapour.

$$\boxed{\textbf{MOCK TEST 5}}$$

ANSWER KEY															
1.	(d)	6.	(d)	11.	(d)	16.	(b)	21.	(b)	26.	(d)	31.	(d)	36.	(a)
2.	(b)	7.	(d)	12.	(d)	17.	(b)	22.	(d)	27.	(a)	32.	(a)	37.	(c)
3.	(b)	8.	(a)	13.	(d)	18.	(b)	23.	(a)	28.	(b)	33.	(b)	38.	(b)
4.	(b)	9.	(a)	14.	(b)	19.	(a)	24.	(a)	29.	(a)	34.	(b)	39.	(a)
5.	(b)	10.	(b)	15.	(a)	20.	(b)	25.	(b)	30.	(b)	35.	(d)	40.	(d)

1. (d) Types of clothes we wear will change with the change in season. Also variety of fruits and vegetables also change with the change in season. For example mango is a summer fruit and oranges are winter fruits.

2. (b) Sunflower

3. (b) Proteins

4. (b) If there is an emergency we dial 100 to speak to the police.

5. (b) Pongal is a festival celebrated by the people in Chennai.

6. (d) Helpers like milkman, watchman and housekeeper make our lives easy and comfortable. We must respect them.

7. (d) Types of clothes we wear depends on both climate and occaion.

8. (a) On Gandhi Jayanti, people visit Rajghat and offer flower and do prayer.

9. (a) Cricket can be played in playground.

10. (b) Swallowing

11. (d) Lion is a wild and carnivorous animal.

12. (d) A boy gets an electric shock as he touched the switch with wet hand.

13. (a) Television, magazine and radio are means of mass communication.

14. (b) Cotton clothes are used in summers.

15. (a) Brain help us to think.

16. (b) Because air is required for burning.

17. (b) Ice is called the solid state of water.

18. (b) Sea water is not a source of drinking water because sea water is very salty.

19. (a) Lungs are organs of the respiratory system.

20. (b) Fast and strong winds are called storm.

21. (b) Taj Mahal is located in Agra, Uttar Pradesh.

22. (d) A plant can breathe, grow and reproduce as it is a living thing.

23. (a) Dr. APJ Abdul Kalam is known as one of the Presidents of India as well as a famous scientist.

24. (a) Fibres like cotton, jute and silk are called natural fibres because they are not created by man using chemicals.

25. (b) Airways is the fastest but the most expensive mode of transport.

26. (d) Caravan is known as house on wheels.

27. (a) Body temperature.

28. (b) The skeleton system gives shape and support to our body.

29. (a) Windmill shows the direction of the wind.

30. (b) Germs make us ill.

31. (d) We get honey from honey bee.

32. (a) Elephant is a herbivorous animal.

33. (b) In winter season we use room heaters and wear sweaters, caps, gloves and it last from November to February.

34. (b) Air is required to make man fly in air.

35. (d) The given picture represent an Internet — means of communication and a computer — an electronic machine.

36. (a) Sun is the main source of heat and light on earth.

37. (c) Raja is living in a joint family.

38. (b)

39. (a) Roots absorb water from the soil.

40. (d) Coal and petrol cannot be reused again and again.

GENERAL KNOWLEDGE

MOCK TEST 1

ANSWER KEY

1	(a)	6	(d)	11	(a)	16	(b)	21	(b)
2	(d)	7	(c)	12	(d)	17	(b)	22	(c)
3	(a)	8	(d)	13	(c)	18	(c)	23	(d)
4	(b)	9	(d)	14	(c)	19	(d)	24	(a)
5	(a)	10	(b)	15	(d)	20	(d)	25	(b)

1. (a) Spinal cord is shown in the given image.

2. (d) Penguin is an aquatic animal.

3. (a) Meat is a body building food.

4. (b) Human body has two lungs.

5. (a) The animal shown in the image is kangaroo which is found in Australia.

6. (d) Tokyo is the capital of Japan.

7. (c) The image shown is the national flag of China.

8. (d) Rafflesia is the largest flower in the world.

9. (d) In place of ball a puck is used in the game of ice hockey.

10. (b) Geeta Phogat is related to wrestling.

11. (a) Mars is also known as the Red Planet.

12. (d) Thiruvananthapuram is the capital of Kerala.

13. (c) Goa is the smallest Indian state in terms of area.

14. (c) Cuckoo does not build its own nest.

15. (d) Pelican has a long pouched beak.

16. (c) Mount everest is the highest mountain.

17. (b) A piece of land that is surrounded by water from all sides is known as island.

18. (c) There are three lights on a traffic signal – yellow, red and green.

19. (d) Before crossing the road, we should always check traffic lights and moving vehicles on both sides of road. We must use zebra crossing.

20. (d) Young one of a monkey is called infant.

21. (b) A net, a racket and a shuttlecock are used in the game of badminton.

22.(c) Jallianwala Bagh massacre took place in Amritsar.

23.(d) Jaipur is also known as 'The Pink City'.

24.(a) Tiger is a 'carnivore' which means it is a meat eating animal.

25.(b) Only statement II is true.

MOCK TEST 2

ANSWER KEY

1	(c)	6	(d)	11	(b)	16	(d)	21	(b)
2	(d)	7	(d)	12	(b)	17	(c)	22	(c)
3	(b)	8	(c)	13	(b)	18	(a)	23	(d)
4	(b)	9	(a)	14	(c)	19	(b)	24	(b)
5	(a)	10	(a)	15	(c)	20	(a)	25	(a)

1. (c) A dry land area with lots of sand, camel and cactus is called desert.

2. (d)

3. (b) Oceans cover more than two third of earth's surface.

4. (b) On a traffic signal, red light indicates stop.

5. (a) Pavements alongside the roads are meant for walking.

6. (d) Traffic rules help us reduce accidents, save lives and avoid traffic jams.

7. (d) In spring season, we see lots of flowers.

8. (c) Trees shed their leaves in autumn.

9. (a) Earth takes one day (24 hours) to complete one rotation around its axis.

10.(a) 'Jana Gana Mana' is the national anthem of India.

11.(b) Humans need oxygen for breathing.

12.(b) Recreation is not a basic need of living beings.

13.(b) Antarctica is known as a cold desert.

14.(c)

15.(c) Australia is a continent that has only one country.

16.(d)

17. (c) Narendra Modi is the Prime Minister of India. He was elected in 2014.

18. (a) Dengue fever is caused by mosquitoes.

19. (b) Hair in nose help in stopping dust to enter our body.

20. (a) Rice and wheat are examples of carbohydrate.

21. (b) Butter is rich in fat.

22. (c) The function of heart in the human body is to pump blood to cells.

23. (d) Mango is the national fruit of India.

24. (b) Only statement II is true.

25. (a) White colour of Indian flag symbolizes peace.

MOCK TEST 3

ANSWER KEY

1	(d)	9	(a)	17	(b)	25	(b)	33	(d)
2	(a)	10	(b)	18	(a)	26	(c)	34	(a)
3	(c)	11	(c)	19	(a)	27	(c)	35	(a)
4	(a)	12	(d)	20	(c)	28	(b)	36	(d)
5	(b)	13	(a)	21	(a)	29	(a)	37	(c)
6	(b)	14	(c)	22	(a)	30	(b)	38	(c)
7	(a)	15	(b)	23	(b)	31	(a)	39	(c)
8	(b)	16	(c)	24	(d)	32	(b)	40	(b)

1. (d) A strip of water having land on two sides is called strait.

2. (a)

3. (c) We should wear seat belts because it's a law that save lives of drivers and passengers.

4. (a) We should use zebra crossing to cross a road.

5. (b) Each season of the year lasts for approximately three months.

6. (b) In winter birds migrate to far off places for food and favourable climate.

7. (a) Seasons happen due to revolution of earth around sun.

8. (b) In winter, some animals hibernate.

9. (a)

10. (b) The earth's spin around its axis is called rotation.

11. (c) If it's day in northern hemisphere, it will be night in southern hemisphere.

12. (d) Plants use carbon dioxide to make food.

13. (a) Plants are necessary for humans because they provide food.

14. (c)

15. (b) Euro is a common currency in most of the countries in Europe.

16. (c) There is no desert in Europe.

17. (b)

18. (a) Temperature of earth would go up if amount of greenhouse gases increases.

19. (a) Athlete's foot disease is caused by fungi.

20. (c) Most of water related diseases are caused by bacteria.

21. (a) Liver is the largest organ in human body.

22. (a) Our lungs are like sponges.

23. (b) Carbon dioxide is thrown out of body by respiratory system.

24. (d) Vitamin helps us in fighting diseases.

25. (b) Fibrous foods are good for our digestive system.

26. (c) Gastric juices are produced in stomach.

27. (c) There are about 300 bones in an infant's body.

28. (b) Heartbeat in children is faster than adults.

29. (a) The study of living beings is known as biology.

30. (b) Size of human heart is equal to person's fist.

31. (a) Core is the innermost layer of earth.

32. (b) It takes sunlight about 8 minutes 20 seconds to reach earth.

33. (d) Earth's pollution is a reason for global warming.

34. (a) Earth is also known as the blue planet.

35. (a) Saffron colour of Indian national flag indicates courage and strength.

36. (d) Banyan is the national tree of India.

37. (c) Sparrow is a grain eating bird with short beak.

38.(c) It's true that every living organism is a part of an ecosystem and habitat is an area where organisms live.

39.(c) Venus is also known as the morning & evening star.

40.(b) Your weight will decrease due to lesser gravity on moon.

MOCK TEST 4

ANSWER KEY

1.	(c)	9.	(a)	17.	(c)	25.	(d)	33.	(a)
2.	(b)	10.	(a)	18.	(a)	26.	(a)	34.	(c)
3.	(c)	11.	(d)	19.	(c)	27.	(b)	35.	(d)
4.	(c)	12.	(d)	20.	(a)	28.	(b)	36.	(b)
5.	(a)	13.	(d)	21.	(b)	29.	(c)	37.	(c)
6.	(c)	14.	(d)	22.	(a)	30.	(d)	38.	(d)
7.	(d)	15.	(b)	23.	(d)	31.	(d)	39.	(d)
8.	(b)	16.	(b)	24.	(c)	32.	(c)	40.	(d)

1. (c) A strip of land having water on two sides is called isthmus.

2. (b) We ski in winter when there is snow all around.

3. (c) The axis of earth is tilted.

4. (c) It's true that animals depend on plants for food. Plants need sunlight to produce food.

5. (a) We get vitamin C from lemon.

6. (c) Half of the world's diamonds are found in Africa.

7. (d) The headquarters of Facebook, Google and Apple are situated in America.

8. (b) There are no towns, villages or cities in Antarctica.

9. (a) Greenhouse effect helps in keeping temperature of earth balanced.

10.(a) Glaciers will melt and there will be more floods if greenhouse gases increase.

11.(d) Carbon dioxide is a greenhouse gas.

12.(d) Malaria is caused by mosquito.

13.(d) Eating street food is a health hazard.

14.(d) Cell is not an example of germ.

15.(b) Some bacteria are helpful in digestion process.

16.(b) Lungs have important role in respiration in human body.

17.(c) Removing waste products from body is the main function of kidneys.

18.(a) Sometimes, we cough while eating food if the food enters windpipe.

19.(c) Protein gives us energy slowly.

20.(a) Banana is a rich source of carbohydrate.

21.(b) Full form of SMS is Short Messaging Service.

22.(a) Saliva is produced in mouth.

23.(d) 50% of our bones are found in our hands and feet.

24.(c) Bones in our shoulder are also known as collar bones.

25.(d) Calcium plays an important role in making our bones stronger.

26.(a) Our heart gets oxygen from lungs.

27.(b) Teeth not only help you eat, but they also help you talk.

28.(b) Canine type of teeth help in tearing.

29.(c) A small child normally has 20 milk teeth.

30.(d) Teeth do not help us in breathing.

31.(d) Konark Sun Temple is situated in Odisha.

32.(c) The constitution of India was written by Dr Bhimrao Ambedkar.

33.(a) Ganga is the national river of India.

34.(c) Bodh Gaya in Bihar is related to Lord Gautam Buddha.

35.(d) Ranchi is capital of Jharkhand.

36.(b) Australian dollar is the currency of Australia.

37.(c) Weaver bird makes a nest shaped flask with mouth at bottom.

38.(d) Eagle has a strong curved beak to tear flesh.

39.(d) Jim Corbett National Park is situated in Uttarakhand.

40.(d) Factories is not a component of ecosystem.

MOCK TEST 5

ANSWER KEY

1	(d)	9	(d)	17	(d)	25	(d)	33	(d)
2	(a)	10	(c)	18	(b)	26	(c)	34	(b)
3	(d)	11	(a)	19	(d)	27	(a)	35	(a)
4	(a)	12	(c)	20	(c)	28	(b)	36	(d)
5	(a)	13	(b)	21	(a)	29	(a)	37	(b)
6	(a)	14	(d)	22	(c)	30	(b)	38	(a)
7	(d)	15	(b)	23	(b)	31	(c)	39	(a)
8	(b)	16	(c)	24	(a)	32	(c)	40	(b)

1. **(d)** It's false that sun is not a part of any ecosystem. Jupiter is the largest planet.

2. **(a)** Mercury is the smallest planet.

3. **(d)** The given image shows lungs.

4. **(a)** Sparrow is an aerial animal.

5. **(a)** Night blindness is caused by deficiency of vitamin A.

6. **(a)** The human body has one liver.

7. **(d)** The animal in image is giraffe which is found in South Africa.

8. **(b)** Beijing is the capital of China.

9. **(d)** The image shown is the national flag of UK.

10. **(c)** Qutab Minar at Delhi was built by Qutubuddin Aibak.

11. **(a)** The sportsperson shown in the image is badminton player Saina Nehwal.

12. **(c)** Children's Day is celebrated on 14th November.

13. **(b)** One US dollar is equal to approximately 65 rupees.

14. **(d)** A person who sells medicines is called a pharmacist.

15. **(b)** Full form of IPL is Indian Premier League.

16. **(c)** Kaziranga National Park is in Assam.

17. **(d)** There are 29 states in India.

18. **(b)** Asthma is a disease of lungs.

19. **(d)** There are 11 players in a football team.

20. **(c)** Jam is made from fruits.

21. **(a)** School is different from the other three.

22. **(c)** A figure with 4 sides is called a rectangle.

23. **(b)** Delhi is situated on the bank of river Yamuna.

24. **(a)** A place where birds are kept is called aviary.

25. **(d)** There are 3600 seconds in an hour.

26. (c) Butter and ghee are rich in fat.

27. (a) Glucose provides instant energy.

28. (b) Most of the harmful bacteria present in food are killed in stomach.

29. (a) The outermost layer of tooth is called enamel.

30. (b) The monument shown in the image is Hawa Mahal, Jaipur.

31. (c) Both statements I and II are correct.

32. (c) This option matches states and capitals correctly.

33. (d) Neptune is farthest from the sun.

34. (b) C. Rajagopalachari was the first Governor General of independent India.

35. (a) Hydrilla is an aquatic plant.

36. (d) Flower of a plant grows into a fruit.

37. (b) Amritsar is known as 'The Golden City'.

38. (a) 'Bharatnatyam' dance is associated with Tamil Nadu.

39. (a) Neerja won National Film Award 2017 for best film in Hindi.

40. (b) 'Eiffel Tower' is located in Paris.

LOGICAL REASONING

MOCK TEST 1

ANSWER KEY

1	(d)	7	(b)	13	(d)	19	(d)	25	(a)
2	(b)	8	(a)	14	(d)	20	(a)	26	(b)
3	(a)	9	(c)	15	(d)	21	(d)	27	(c)
4	(d)	10	(a)	16	(b)	22	(c)	28	(b)
5	(c)	11	(b)	17	(c)	23	(b)	29	(d)
6	(b)	12	(c)	18	(d)	24	(b)	30	(b)

1. (d) The bottle has a lid (cap) to close unlike in the other three.

2. (b) The 2nd figure fits exactly into the first.

3. (a) We get each next number by adding 10 in its previous.

$$\underbrace{21 \quad 31 \quad 41 \quad 51 \quad \boxed{61}}_{+10 \quad\ +10 \quad\ +10 \quad\ +10}$$

4. (d) All four sticks start from same point.

Hence, Q is the longest stick.

5. (c) Straight lines : PQ, QR, RS, ST, TU, UV, VW, WX, XY, YZ, ZD, DE, PE.

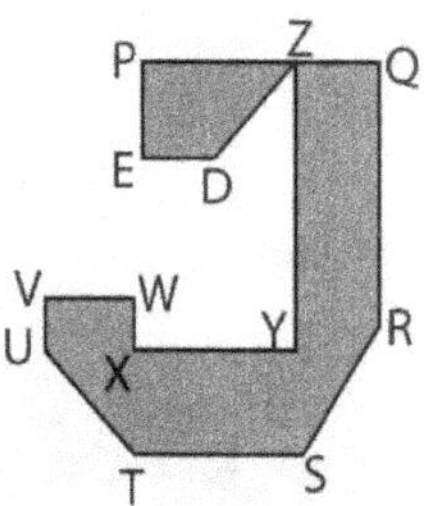

6. (b) Option (b) has the hidden part.

7. (b).

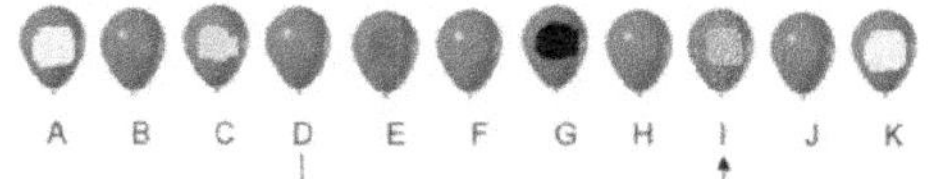

8. (a) Milk is of white colour and white is called black.

9. (c) A car has = 4 wheels

4 cars have = 4 + 4 + 4 + 4 = 16

A scooter has = 2 wheels

2 scooter have = 2 + 2 = 4

Total wheels = 16 + 4 = 20

10. (a) There are total 16 items in the given picture.

11. (b) There 9 items between pen and alarm.

12. (c) BCDA is the proper sequence.

13. (d) Each figure repeats itself after 3 figures.

14. (d) Triangles : T_1, T_2, T_3, T_4, T_5, T_6 and big triangle.

15. (d) As,

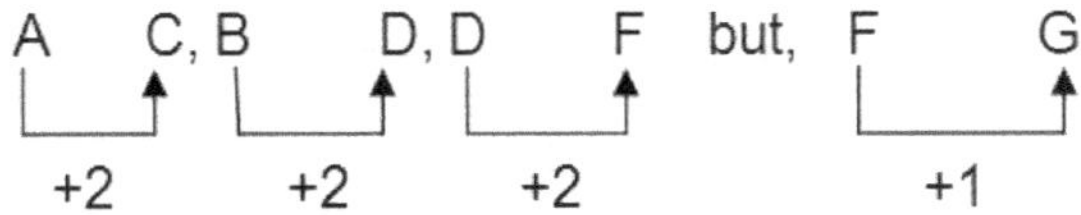

16. (b) Toy Q

17. (c) All the things except the umbrella are used for cleaning.

18. (d) The pattern repeats for every three objects.

19. (d) First figure rotates vertically upwards.

20. (a) 4 groups of 5 apples (if there are 4 apples in each plate) can be formed from given apples.

21. (d) (Rank of Kavya from the top + Rank of Kavya from the bottom) – 1

$= (10 + 4) - 1$

$= 14 - 1$

$= 13$

22. (c) As, $\overset{M \quad A \quad N}{\underset{O \quad B \quad P}{+2 \ +1 \ +2}}$ Similarly $\overset{S \quad U \quad N}{\underset{U \quad V \quad P}{+2 \ +1 \ +2}}$

23. (b) Shape given in option (b) is hidden in the figure as shown below

So, option (b) is correct.

24. (b) Lova is tallest and Mio is shortest among them.

Sol. 25 to 27

Ana > Kaka > Mahi > Nanu

25. (a) Ana is tallest among them.

26. (b) Mahi is between Kaka and Nanu.

27. (c) Nanu is shortest among them.

28. (b) PSRQ is the proper sequence.

29. (d) Height of all the beakers are same but width of beaker S is maximum.

30. (b) The pattern is as follows:

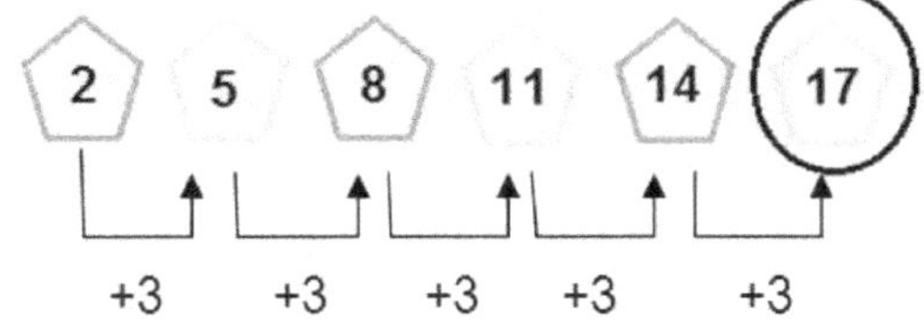

MOCK TEST 2

ANSWER KEY

1	(b)	7	(b)	13	(a)	19	(c)	25	(b)
2	(d)	8	(a)	14	(b)	20	(c)	26	(d)
3	(b)	9	(c)	15	(b)	21	(d)	27	(c)
4	(a)	10	(d)	16	(b)	22	(d)	28	(c)
5	(b)	11	(b)	17	(d)	23	(c)	29	(b)
6	(b)	12	(c)	18	(b)	24	(d)	30	(d)

1. **(b)** The pattern is as follows:

$$A \xrightarrow{+2} C \xrightarrow{+2} E \xrightarrow{+2} G \xrightarrow{+2} \text{(I)}$$

2. **(d)** Squares: A, B, C, D, E, F, G, H, I and big square.

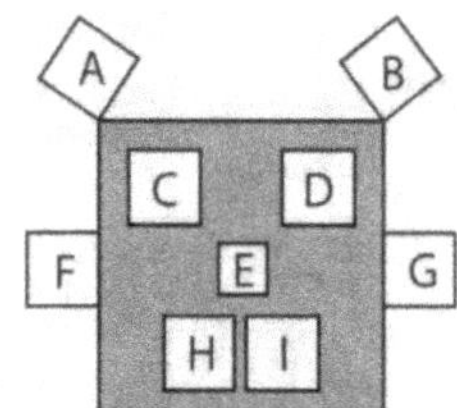

3. **(b)** Brushing teeth, washing hands and bathing all are good habits.

4. **(a)** Ant P is fifth from left end.

5. **(b)** Ant C is fourth to the right of ant M.

6. **(b)** If Ant R and E interchange their positions, then Ant E is at left end.

7. **(b)** There are 4 triangles in the figure.

8. **(a)** ![G] is shortest among them.

9. **(c)** Option (c) is correct.

10. **(d)** Fingers is the part of hand but hand is called hair.

11. **(b)** There are 2 children in the garden.

12. **(c)** There are 2 animals in the garden.

13. **(a)** Only 1 bird is flying in the sky.

14. **(b)** Option (b) is correct answer.

15. **(b)** 45 is greater than 20 .

16. **(c)** The month whose name begins with A is the 4th month of the year. It has 30 days in a month.

17. **(d)** 2300 m = 2 km 300 m.

18. **(b)** In option (b), table is heavier than all.

19. **(c)** As, $24 = 2 + 4 = 6$

$600 = 6 + 0 + 0 = 6$

$15 = 1 + 5 = 6$

But, $71 = 7 + 1 = 8$

20. **(c)** If he practices for 15 days then his practice finishes on 19th january.

Sol. 21 to 25

The sitting arrangement is as following:

Q   P   R   S

21. (d) S

22. (d) R

23. (c) PR

24. (d) Q

25. (b) P

26. (d) There are 6 stairs in between 5th stair and 12th stair.

27. (c) BEDCA is the correct sequence.

28. (c) 3+4=7, 7+4=11, 11+4=15, 15+4=19, 19+4=23

29. (b) There are 5 circles in the figure.

30. (d) The weight of a scooter will be 100-120kg.

MOCK TEST 3

ANSWER KEY

1	(b)	7	(c)	13	(b)	19	(b)	25	(a)
2	(b)	8	(a)	14	(a)	20	(b)	26	(c)
3	(a)	9	(c)	15	(c)	21	(a)	27	(d)
4	(a)	10	(b)	16	(a)	22	(b)	28	(b)
5	(d)	11	(b)	17	(a)	23	(c)	29	(d)
6	(d)	12	(a)	18	(a)	24	(b)	30	(c)

1. (b) A person sits on chair and chair is called table.

2. (b) After each step their is addition of 1 part.

3. (a) Number of rectangles is 5. Number of circles is 6. Therefore there are 1 circles more than rectangles.

4. (a) The figure in option (a) has the question figure hidden in it.

5. (d) The pattern has four continuous numbers with each number starting with a number 1 less than the previous one.

Sol. 6 to 8

Sitting arrangement

Left   Right

Bunny   Anil   Chetan   Divansh

6. (d) Divansh is sitting at the right corner.

7. (c) Anil and Chetan are sitting in the middle.

8. (a) Anil is sitting at the second position from the left.

9. (c) Except option (c), in all others first and third digits are same.

10. (b) All except (b) are filled with colour.

11. (b) The 2nd figure fits exactly into the first.

19. (b) String Q is straight and string R is more curved than string P. Hence R, is longest and Q is shortest.

20. (b) Number in second row is obtained by adding number of the first row 3 times.

$6 = 2 + 2 + 2$, $\boxed{9} = 3 + 3 + 3$.

21. (a) Each figure repeats itself after three figures.

22. (b) On observing the given letters, we can see the correct word is SCALE.

23. (c) As,

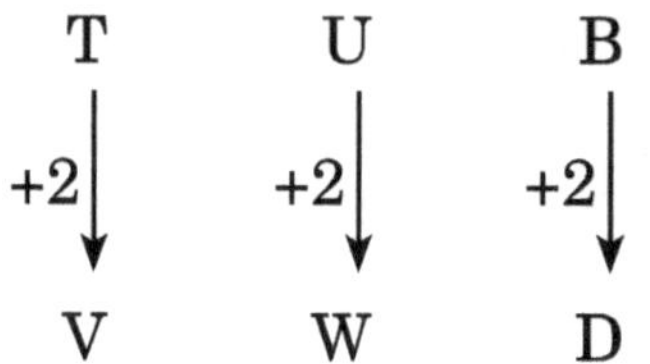

Similarly,

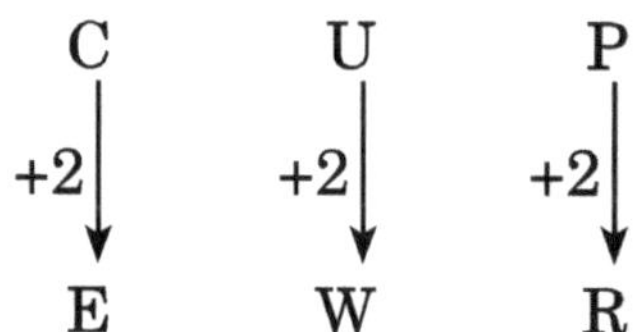

24. (b) There are total 10 fruits in the picture.

25. (a) There are 3 red-coloured fruits in the picture.

26. (c) There are 2 green-coloured fruits in the picture.

27. (d) There are 7 fruits in between pineapple and apple.

28. (b) 6 is shortest among them.

29. (d) $30 > 15 < 27$ is correct.

30. (c) The figure is made up of 6 circles.

MOCK TEST 4

ANSWER KEY

1	(a)	6	(a)	11	(a)	16	(d)	21	(d)
2	(c)	7	(d)	12	(d)	17	(c)	22	(b)
3	(c)	8	(d)	13	(a)	18	(b)	23	(c)
4	(c)	9	(d)	14	(b)	19	(d)	24	(d)
5	(d)	10	(d)	15	(d)	20	(d)	25	(b)

1. (a) Number in ☐ is obtained by adding number in △ two times.

$20 = 10 + 10$, $10 = 5 + 5$

2. (c) 3 & 6 figure is combined figure of (1, 2) & (4, 5). The uncoloured part of the figure becomes coloured and vice – versa.

3. (c) Number of teddy bears in Pattern 4 = 10

Number of teddy bears in Pattern 2 = 3

Number of teddy bear in Pattern 3 = 5

$$1 \quad 3 \quad 5 \quad 7 \quad \boxed{9}$$
$$+2 \quad +2 \quad +2 \quad +2$$

4. (c) 2413221 2413221

2413221 2413 | 3 |

5. (d) X = W, W is lighter than Z, X is heavier than Y. The order from the heaviest to the lightest is Z, W, X, Y or Z, X, W, Y

6. (a) 4 kettles filled up 1 pail,

$4 + 4 + 4 + 4 + 4 = 20$ kettles filled 5 pails.

7. (d) Triangles : T_1, T_2, T_3, T_4, T_5

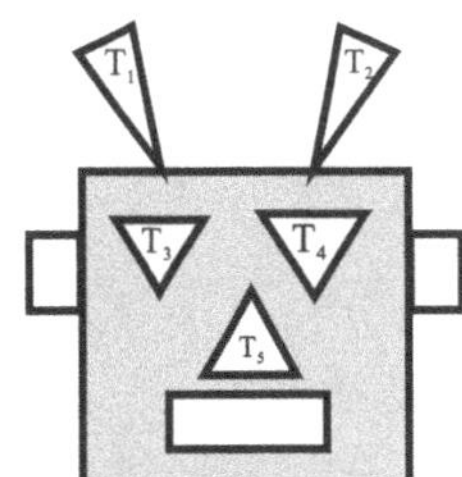

8. (d)

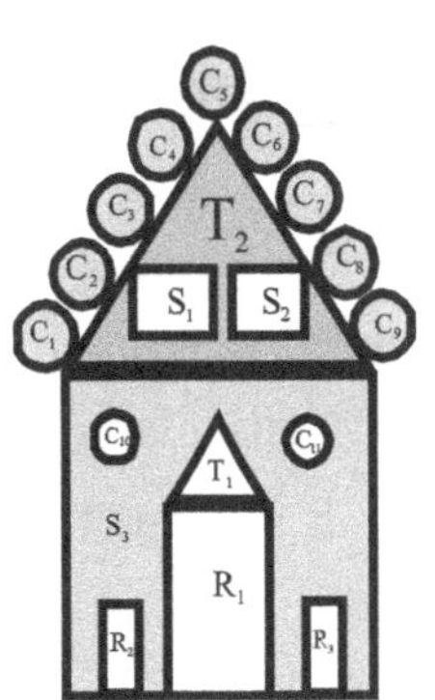

9. (d) Objects in (a), (b) and (c) are musical instruments.

10. (d) In (a), (b) and (c) inner figure are divided in equal parts.

11. (a) One more same figure is added of different colour and size is reduced.

18. (b) King of jungle is lion and lion is called rabbit.

19. (d) Only in (d) the question figure appears exactly.

20. (d) From left bottom to right top, the letters are in a sequence.

21. (d) C, E, B, A, D is the correct sequence.

22. (b) There are 4 balloons in the picture.

23. (c) There are 5 candles on the cake in the picture.

Sol. 24 & 25

Avika > Shalu > Pari > Nikita

24. (d) Nikita is shortest among them.

25. (b) Avika is tallest among them.

MOCK TEST 5

ANSWER KEY

1	(b)	6	(b)	11	(d)	16	(c)	21	(b)
2	(d)	7	(b)	12	(c)	17	(d)	22	(a)
3	(a)	8	(d)	13	(b)	18	(c)	23	(c)
4	(b)	9	(a)	14	(a)	19	(b)	24	(d)
5	(a)	10	(d)	15	(d)	20	(d)	25	(b)

1. (b) Middle number is obtained by multiplying top and bottom numbers.

Therefore $11 \times 3 = 33$

2. (d) Each figure repeats itself after 3 figure.

3. (a) Number of flowers in pattern 1 = 4

Number of flower in pattern 2 = 6

Number of flower in pattern 3 = 8

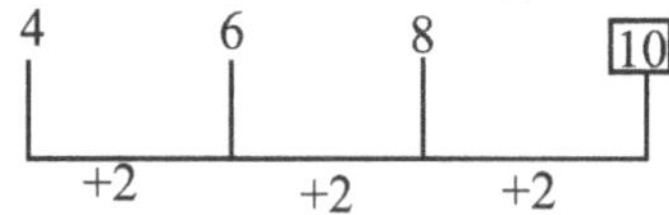

Number of flowers in pattern 4 = 10

4. (b) ABCBDD ABCBDD

ABCBDD AB

5. (a) $3X = 1Y$ amd $1X = 2W$

$\Rightarrow 1Y = 6W$

7. (b) Triangles : T_1, T_2, T_3, T_4, T_5, T_6, T_7, T_8, T_9, T_{10}

Circles : C_1, C_2

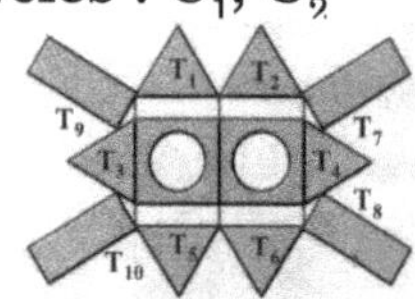

9. (a) Objects in (b), (c) and (d) are the media operators.

10. (d) Figures in (a), (b) and (c) are formed only by curved lines.

11. (d) All the elements are placed separately.

16. (c) Because there are 14 triangles in given figure.

18. (c) Second day of week is Monday and Monday is called Tuesday.

19. (b) The figure in option (b) has exactly the same shapes as the question figure.

20. (d)

N	O	P	Q
M	X	Y	R
L	W	Z	S
K	V	U	T

21. (b) She wears middy after 3 hours.

22. (a) She wears long suit at 12:00 noon.

23. (c) $54 < 62 > 23 < 78$ is correct.

24. (d) The figure is made up of 4 triangles and 7 circles.

25. (b) 1, 4, 2, 5, 3 is the correct sequence.

CYBER

MOCK TEST 1

ANSWER KEY

1	(d)	6	(b)	11	(c)	16	(d)	21	(d)
2	(d)	7	(a)	12	(a)	17	(b)	22	(a)
3	(a)	8	(b)	13	(d)	18	(d)	23	(d)
4	(d)	9	(c)	14	(b)	19	(b)	24	(c)
5	(a)	10	(a)	15	(c)	20	(a)	25	(a)

1. **(d)** All the given devices are based on smart computer based machine.

3. **(a)** ALU is the part of CPU (Central processing unit). It can be used to perform arithmetical and logical operations.

5. **(a)** A minicomputer is not a portable computer because it takes more space than micro-computer or personal computer.

6. **(b)** A motherboard (sometimes known as the main-board, system board, baseboard, planar board or logic board) is the main printed circuit board (PCB) found in general purpose microcomputers and other expandable systems.

8. **(b)** (i) UPS and (ii) Power supply unit

10. **(a)** Only mouse and keyboard are input devices and all other are output devices.

11. **(c)** A personal computer (PC) is an inexpensive microcomputer originally designed to be used by only one person at a time.

16. **(d)** All three of them are used to enter data into the computer.

20. **(a)** Open curves

22. **(a)** To use the different kind of brushes, go to Home tab-Brushes group.

23. **(d)** An app is a program designed for users. For example Whatsapp, Facebook App, etc.

25. **(a)** Windows 10

Windows XP Professional	25 April 2005
Windows Vista	30 Jan, 2007
Windows 7	22 Oct, 2009
Windows 8	26 Oct, 2012
Windows 8.1	17 Oct, 2013
Windows 10	29 July, 2015

MOCK TEST 2

ANSWER KEY									
1	(a)	6	(a)	11	(d)	16	(c)	21	(c)
2	(b)	7	(c)	12	(d)	17	(c)	22	(d)
3	(d)	8	(c)	13	(a)	18	(c)	23	(d)
4	(a)	9	(b)	14	(c)	19	(a)	24	(d)
5	(b)	10	(d)	15	(b)	20	(a)	25	(c)

1. (a) Among the given options, only option (a), is a smart phone, and it is a hand-held device that can be connected to the computer with the help of data cable.

2. (b) Mainframe is a powerful multi-user computer capable of supporting many hundreds or thousands of users simultaneously.

3. (d) Supercomputer is an extremely fast computer that can perform hundreds of millions of instructions per second.

6. (a) By keeping it in a cool and dust free room.

8. (c) (i) Floppy disk and (ii) RAM

13. (a) In modern computer systems, backspace moves the cursor one position backwards and deletes the character at that position, and shifts back the text after that position by one position.

14. (c) It opens the start menu

15. (b) Spacebar is the longest key on the keyboard.

16. (c) Clicking and dragging

17. (c) Left click on this icon

21. (c) Mouse pad is made of rubber or foam.

25. (c) Angry Birds

MOCK TEST 3

ANSWER KEY

1	(d)	6	(c)	11	(d)	16	(b)	21	(b)
2	(d)	7	(a)	12	(a)	17	(b)	22	(c)
3	(a)	8	(b)	13	(a)	18	(a)	23	(c)
4	(b)	9	(c)	14	(d)	19	(a)	24	(b)
5	(c)	10	(c)	15	(a)	20	(d)	25	(d)

1. (d) The jumbled words are

(a) RIGID   (b) DUMB

(c) SLOW   (d) SMART

Hence, the correct answer is option (d).

2. (d) Both (a) and (b). Both are the Google map, which are application softwares used to search direction while traveling.

4. (b) BIOS (basic input output system) is the program a computer microprocessor uses to get the computer system started after you turn it on. It also manages data flow between the computer's operating system and attached devices such as the hard disk, video adapter, keyboard, mouse and printer.

8. (b) The jumbled word is MONITOR. Hence, both 1 and 2 are correct.

9. (c) (i) Heat Sink Processor Fan and (ii) Hard disk

14.(d) It will move the cursor to the end of the line.

19.(a) It is known as free form selection, and it is used to select the desired shape of the images.

20.(d) Option (d) is known as invert selection as it is not used for deleting the selected object.

22.(c) Candy crush jelly saga

23.(c) Android operating system

25.(d) An iPod is a small portable media player produced by Apple Inc.